# THE GUIDE TO SUCCESSFUL CONSUMER BANKING STRATEGY

# THE GUIDE TO SUCCESSFUL CONSUMER BANKING STRATEGY

### ROBERT G. STEMPER

**WILEY**

## John Wiley & Sons
New York • Chichester • Brisbane • Toronto • Singapore

**Library of Congress Cataloging-in-Publication Data**

Stemper, Robert G.
    The guide to successful consumer banking strategy / by Robert G.
Stemper.
        p.     cm.
    Bibliography:  p.
    Includes index.
    ISBN 0-471-50112-3
    1. Bank management.   2. Consumer credit.   I. Title.
HG1615.S754    1989
332.1′7′068—dc19                                                        89-5484
                                                                              CIP

Printed in the United States of America

10   9   8   7   6   5   4   3   2   1

To George, Catherine,
and Florence with much love.

# CONTENTS

## Culture Can Kill

# LIST OF GUIDES

# INTRODUCTION

This book will help you get on the critical path to success. Whether you are currently managing a consumer bank, would like to do so, or need to know more about consumer banking, I have identified seven essential principles for success based on my 20 years' experience in the industry and thousands of conversations with customers and bank employees. The customers varied from people who only cashed a check to those who wanted to borrow tens of millions of dollars to buy a business. The bank employees were everyone from tellers to CEOs, at commercial banks, savings banks, and savings and loan associations. The principles can help you identify what issues you should address to be successful.

Some key concepts behind the principles are:

- *Expenses are resources to achieve the vision.* Expense control is critical to successfully managing a business. The question is how to do it. The answer is to view expenses as resources to achieve the vision of the bank. Review all the expenses: people, operating expenses, and capital budget. If the expense is essential in achieving the vision, we need it, or we need a new vision. If the expense is not essential, we should probably eliminate it. By following this approach, we may find several items that can be eliminated and other areas where spending should be increased to the critical level necessary to achieve the vision. I like to keep in mind the story of the time Albert Einstein was hired but then denied his request for a blackboard. Either he should not have been hired or he should have been supplied with a blackboard. Banks often find themselves in this no-win middle ground in managing expenses.

- *Service is a partnership with the customer.* The customer not only participates with the bank in the "manufacture" of service, but also makes a judgment on how effective it is. So first find out how the customer judges service. Some customers judge by efficiency, others by expertise, and still others by convenience of banking hours. Once service is defined, we have a focus and can work with customers to determine how they would like to participate in the "manufacture" of the service. Perhaps it's via a telephone, a PC or face-to-face.

- *Consumer banking is really three different businesses.* If we estimate the profit that each household in a given market generates for the financial service industry and then assign each household to a low, medium, or high profit group, we will find that the averages for each group are far apart. The management issues and actions that are appropriate for one group may not be for another. For example, in the low profit group, slight changes in revenue or expenses may make the group unprofitable. The issue here may be to reduce expenses while still meeting customers' needs. In the high profit group, slight changes in the revenue or expenses may not significantly impact profitability, and certainly will not make these customers unprofitable. The issue here may be to increase expenses to better meet their needs and get more of their business.

- *There are only four possible strategies for managing a consumer bank.* If you accept the idea that the mission of the consumer banking industry is to profitably satisfy customers' needs, then there really are only two possible dimensions to strategic options: customers and needs. We can plan on satisfying all needs of all customers; all needs of some customers; some needs of all customers; or some needs for some customers. If, after analyzing the options, we select some customers, some needs, we will want to make sure that our actions are consistent with that strategy—for instance, by investing resources only in programs that serve our selected needs in our target market.

- *The customer contact staff largely regulates bank profitability.* The human being who interfaces with a customer may be 0 to 100 percent efficient at any given time. That person may be setting the standards for excellence one day and not meeting any of them the next. This variability affects the customer and, in turn, the bank's profit, so focusing on the contact staff as the regulator of profit has some big rewards.

- *Management's primary role is supporting the customer's interface with the bank.* The customer is the source of revenue for the bank; hence the bank's interaction with the customer should be the focus of management and its primary role. If the customer uses an ATM, some of the relevant issues for management are human factors, design, uptime, hours of access, and menus of transactions. If the customer interfaces with a bank employee, we want to ensure that the employee has the appropriate tools, training, and motivation to maximize revenue and profit.

- *The biggest problem some banks have is consistency between word and action.* If bank management says cross-selling is important but doesn't know how many sales each banker makes or how many products each customer has, how important can it be? This inconsistency has some major implications. For one thing, it introduces a noise level in communication where the employees begin to feel they don't know what the real message is unless they can relate it to a past action. As a result, the past action conveys the message. It also can gradually destroy the trust employees have in management, and trust is the magic ingredient in an effective organization.

- *An effective sales program is an interrelated effort fundamentally dependent on maintaining a sales culture.* The culture in the bank must first say that selling is important if it is to become important. Management can work to create this culture not only by providing all the needed tools, training, and incentives, but also by being a cheerleader, facilitator, and supporter of the sales effort. Once the right culture is present, we can start looking at sales as a system to make sure all the required components are in place and working together.

As important as concepts are in building a framework to permit one to independently understand a subject, they take on added importance when coupled with guides to action. The guides in this book are stand-alone pages that can be easily referenced and applied to particular issues. Some of the key guides to action include:

- *Employee charter.* What better way to recognize and release the potential of each employee than by giving each one his or her own charter? The charter defines the employee's role in accomplishing the mission of the bank and his or her authority to do so.

- *Estimating profit potential.* Managing a business without knowing the profit potential is like buying a lottery ticket without knowing the prize. A process to analyze a market and develop effective need-satisfying products is essential for estimating profit potential. This process identifies the data required, how to acquire the data, and the creative process involved.

- *Customer's bill of rights.*   A sample bill of rights clearly spells out what customers can expect from the bank. It sets a tone for the relationship with the bank. In the intangible world of service, this is essential.

- *Customer contract.*   For each product, the customer receives a document that not only spells out the bank's rights and responsibilities, but also the customer's rights and responsibilities. As a buyer, each customer should have this right.

- *Danger signs of culture.*   This is a checklist that will help you determine if the right culture, one that supports the mission and vision of the bank, is in place. It also can be used as a guide to putting the right culture for your bank in place.

- *Manager's creed.*   This provides each manager with a practical day-to-day guide. It facilitates independent action that is consistent with the business and is brief enough so that it can be really used.

- *Turning customers into clients.*   How do clients differ from customers? Clients are like money in the bank—they just continue to grow if they are managed correctly. One of the chapters in this book talks about how to do this.

- *Opportunity test.*   This test lists the relevant questions to address when considering a new product idea. It can help prevent decisions that could be damaging to the business and one's career.

- *The three essential reports needed to manage the business.*   Banks are often awash in reports, but there are three reports that are essential to managing the execution of the bank's mission. One is a customer service report monitoring the delivery of service in terms of how the customers define service. The second is a report that measures individual customer profitability. The third is a market share report that tracks over time how successful a bank is vis-à-vis the competitors.

The concepts and guides work together toward a single purpose: to help you better understand how to manage a consumer bank by keeping you on the critical path to success.

The first chapter in this book, "Seven Principles for Successfully Managing a Consumer Bank," provides a framework for thought and action and should be read first. After that, pick a chapter that is relevant at the moment and you are on your way to success.

# ACKNOWLEDGMENTS

Many people were helpful in writing this book. Although I have never met some of them, I have been influenced by their writings, which are included in the bibliography.

Many people were instrumental in shaping my views when I worked for Citibank and Chase Manhattan Bank. I would particularly like to thank Charles E. Long, executive vice president, Citibank; Paul Kolterjohn, senior vice president (retired), Citibank; and Therese M. Molloy, vice president (retired), Chase.

Two people I worked closely with for several years were instrumental in crystallizing my ideas about branch managers and relationship officers. They are James A. Handal, vice president, and Eileen Hunt Barrett, second vice president (retired), both with Chase.

In discussing the idea for a book, everyone I spoke to added some value; four people had piercing insights into the nature of the business: Richard S. Braddock, sector executive, Citibank; Arthur J. Ryan, vice chairman, Chase; Patrick M. Keane, executive vice president, First Fidelity Bank, NA, New Jersey; and Charles J. Hamm, president and CEO, Independence Savings Bank.

The book would not be as readable as it is without the critical feedback of two friends and former colleagues: Babette A. Basil and Cynthia J. Miller, both vice presidents at Citibank.

Many people were generous with their time and ideas in reviewing the book in its various stages. They include W. James Tozer, Jr., president and chief operating officer, Prudential-Bache,

Inc., Arthur J. Bassin, executive vice president, The Dime Savings Bank of New York, FSB; George R. Kabureck, president and chief operating officer, Northeast Bancorp, Inc.; Evan Juro, Evan Juro Associates; Ronald J. Koprowski, formerly vice president, Chase; John C. Reinertsen, principal, Judd-Falk, Inc.; Harry W. Rivkin, formerly president, Accountline Financial Services, Inc.

People who are familiar with my handwriting know the importance of Mary Humphrey, who typed the manuscript.

I would also like to thank John Wiley & Sons for publishing the book, particularly Karl Weber for his guidance and support and Pat Stahl for making my words more intelligible. Without them the book would not have been published.

R.G.S.

# KEYS TO SUCCESS

# Seven Principles for Success

---

1. Consumer banks have interrelated parts.

2. Vision drives the bank.

3. Profitably satisfying customers' needs frames the mission.

4. Customer interaction is the key to the business.

5. The contact staff and the product offering regulate profitability.

6. Survival requires innovation.

7. Culture can kill.

# Chapter 1

# Seven Principles for Successfully Managing a Consumer Bank

The most important decision any manager faces is what issues to address and what to do. Selecting the right issues and managing them effectively are keys to success. In consumer banking there are seven essential principles for selecting the right issues and managing them. These principles define the critical path to success.

## PRINCIPLE 1: CONSUMER BANKS HAVE INTERRELATED PARTS

From a customer's point of view, a bank is a mix of products, services, and distribution systems that satisfy his or her financial needs. From the bank's perspective it's even more complex. There are sellers and tellers, people who communicate with customers, process their checks, set their rates, replenish the ATMs, design new distribution systems—the list could go on and on. All these efforts work in concert to satisfy customers' financial needs. In fact, the interrelated parts are a system. The danger is managing them as if they were unrelated, as the new marketing director at one bank found out.

   The individual had an impressive background in marketing and in his last position had substantially increased the sales of his business. He was hired to do the same thing for the bank.

Before long, he made a presentation to senior management about his sales program. He decided to concentrate on one product for his first campaign. Goals had been set for each branch based on the market potential, size of the branch, and past performance. The marketing director had tested the product delivery system by opening about a hundred accounts and thoroughly exercising the product features. He made sure that the sales staff was familiar with the product and had whatever sales support was required. An advertising agency developed the communication program; the bank held a sales rally to kick off the program and offered an incentive program for the staff. In short, everything was done to ensure that sales would increase, and indeed they did.

The problem surfaced when the financials for the quarterly report were being prepared. Expenses had gone up due to the sales campaign but were still slightly under forecast. Revenue, however, had taken a nose dive. After some analysis, the bank determined that it had lost more than its normal number of customers and that some of them were its most profitable customers. The sales staff was so focused on selling that one product that they ignored their existing customers. After several weeks of this, the better customers just left.

Sales are important, but the bank had forgotten that the bottom line is profitably satisfying customers' needs over time, and servicing existing accounts and relationships is an essential part of doing that. They forgot that banking is a system of inter-related parts.

This case study illustrates that before changing one part of the system to understand how that change will affect the rest of the system, we must:

- Identify all the systemic elements that are related to achieving a particular objective.

- Manage each element individually.

- Make sure they work together.

## PRINCIPLE 2: VISION DRIVES THE BANK

Most people would not get in a car without knowing where they are headed. Banks, too, need a vision of where they are going. The vision should be a word picture of what the bank will look like when it gets there. It should describe the bank from both the bank's point of view and the customer's.

A vision provides a guide to action for the bank and a sense of what lies ahead for the customer. The CEO of one consumer bank had a clear vision of where he wanted to take the bank, but he had not done a very effective job of communicating that vision to the directors, the consumers, or the staff. He expended a lot of emotional energy and bank resources, but no one really knew what he wanted. More and more decisions wound up in his lap, until he reached overload and nothing got done. This turned off the staff, and they turned off the customers.

Let's assume we avoid that problem by molding a vision in a collegial fashion and selling it to our constituencies. Where do we go from here? We use that vision as a guide in allocating resources. Everything we do should be tested against the vision. The *we* here refers to everyone in the bank. Everyone has to be on board and pulling in the same direction if the consumer banking system is to work successfully. Yes, vision drives the bank, but it has to be well communicated, and unity is essential.

## PRINCIPLE 3: PROFITABLY SATISFYING CUSTOMERS' NEEDS FRAMES THE MISSION

While the vision describes how a bank will look and feel, a mission is more specific. It indicates what has to be done—in this case, profitably satisfying customers' needs.

The mission reflects what the customer is buying—satisfaction—and suggests that this won't happen in a free economy unless the supplier makes a profit. But there are some implications of the mission that we will want to explore.

Ideally, we would like to satisfy customers' needs over time. Repeat business with the same customers is more profitable in the short run and usually builds a more viable business over time. So the mission statement will have both short- and long-term implications.

The mission is to serve *each* customer's needs profitably, not to serve the needs of *all* customers as a group. This may sound like a semantic distinction, but it's not; it's fundamental to successfully managing the bank. The fact that a consumer bank is profitable as an entity doesn't mean that every customer is profitable. In fact, many banks don't know the profitability of their own customers.

If profit is measured at the institutional rather than the individual customer level, the bank is probably managed the same way; that is, few if any customer differences are recognized. If customers were alike in terms of needs and profit potential, this might be acceptable, but they are not. If you look at the 20 percent of the most profitable customers in your bank, they probably as a group have an average profit of five to ten times that of the average customer (with the high profit group included). The high profit group also uses more and different types of products than the average customer. Clearly, then, there are significant business reasons for ensuring that the mission statement means *each* customer should have his or her needs profitably served.

The mission statement forms the basis for successful business management, so it is important to craft it very carefully. Out of the mission statement emerge the basic issues for successful management.

- Focusing on the customer
- Managing the current customer mix profitably
- Developing the essential management information systems to monitor the business
- Understanding the four core strategies for success in the consumer banking business

- Leveraging current customers to higher levels of profitability
- Researching and identifying new customers
- Segmenting the market
- Establishing an appropriate organizational structure
- Identifying key roles in the bank

All of these issues will be discussed in upcoming chapters.

## PRINCIPLE 4: CUSTOMER INTERACTION IS THE KEY TO THE BUSINESS

Customers provide revenue. The satisfaction that customers are buying takes place when they interact with the bank by getting cash, obtaining a mortgage, or using a safe-deposit box. This means that the success or failure of the bank happens at the point where customers interact with the bank. If we are opening a new consumer bank today, this fact would probably be taken for granted. However, most managers are associated with existing banks. Because most banks were established in an era of strict federal regulation, they tend to focus on the demands of regulators rather than the needs of customers. That mind-set has to change in today's competitive, deregulated banking environment.

So the real issue with principle 4 is not convincing people that it is true, but getting people to act on their beliefs. As George Bernard Shaw once said, "The only problem with Christianity is that it's never been tried." Notwithstanding the reluctance to change, what does this principle of customer interaction suggest in terms of action?

- Focus on the customer as the revenue provider.
- Recognize that customers and the bank are partners in the interaction.

7

- Specify that management's principal role is to support customer interactions.

- Provide the contact staff with a seamless, efficient support system to help them meet customers' needs.

- Give the contact staff as much information as possible about customers so that they can satisfy their needs.

- Educate the contact staff about all the products the bank sells as well as its competitors.

- Give all employees a clear and complete charter of their responsibilities and authority.

- Ensure that the manager who directly supervises contact staff is perceived as important by senior management, staff, and customers.

- Recognize that customers form perceptions when they interact with a bank, and manage that process.

- Custom-tailor the bank's communications and actions to suit the differing needs and profit potential of its customers.

- Ensure that senior managers mesh their words and actions because they are often removed from direct interaction with customers.

If the above list seems daunting, it's because managing customer interaction is a complex process. We will discuss each of the above points in subsequent chapters. The objective here is to get a flavor for the overall process.

Although we might recognize the importance of customer interaction, we are often tempted to focus on other aspects of the business, like processing and control. These types of concerns are valid, but we must keep in mind that they support the generation of revenue and the satisfaction of needs that occur when the customer interacts with the bank.

## PRINCIPLE 5: THE CONTACT STAFF AND THE PRODUCT OFFERING REGULATE PROFITABILITY

To put this principle to work, we must first understand how we can affect customers' behavior so they bring us profitable business. The solution lies in understanding how consumers make financial decisions so that we can impact the process. In those instances where consumers do not interface with a bank employee (e.g., when writing a check or using an ATM), the issues we face are largely of a design nature. Since consumers are going to use what we design, we need their ongoing input and feedback. In those instances where the customer does interface with a bank employee, we have the same design issues, but we also have another factor—the human element of the contact staff. This is the most variable of all the variables affecting profitability and need satisfaction. The issue here for managers is how to impact the contact staff.

If we were to analyze a group of branches, we would probably find that the length of time the bank has been in its current location, the customer base it serves, and the size of the branch would explain some of the differences between profitable and unprofitable branches. Other key factors would surface upon further analysis.

First and foremost, we would find that the successful branch manager thinks and acts like an entrepreneur. He or she is focused on making money, not slavishly following dictates from the head office. The manager has figured out how to keep the branch running smoothly, even if it involves a system of his or her own invention.

The staff has been well trained in products, roles, and service. Each member of the branch has a clearly understood role and personal goals that relate to serving customers' needs. The safe-deposit attendant does not merely provide access to the boxes, but actively tries to find new business. No opportunity for customer interaction is missed. The bank manager rewards each employee for individual success in customer satisfaction and profit. The manager sets the

9

example of how to profitably satisfy customers' needs. He or she is visible in the branch and active in identifying new customers.

The bottom line is that the bank manager recognizes that the contact staff regulates profitability and provides valuable feedback on product design. This is an over-arching principle in consumer banking.

## PRINCIPLE 6: SURVIVAL REQUIRES INNOVATION

As the banking industry continues its transition from a regulated to a deregulated environment, all sorts of changes are required, some small, some large. Foremost is focusing on the customers, not the regulators. But other changes are also taking place in the business environment: Customers' needs are changing, the population mix is changing, customers are more knowledgeable and demanding, work ethics are changing. In short, the industry is in a whirlwind of change.

Increased competition for the same consumers means that banks must change if they hope to survive. Innovation is difficult to manage and often hard to measure, but it is necessary for survival. What are some of the parameters for change?

- First is that the culture in the bank must be receptive to it. Management can pinpoint areas where change is required and provide the resources and emotional support to address them, but they cannot accomplish the change by themselves. They have to orchestrate this among the customers and the staff.

- Change involves risk. Management must acknowledge that fact and show a tolerance for risk. By the same token, management has an opportunity to minimize risk by making sure that a new program is well thought out, well researched, well planned, and, above all, well monitored in its execution. If a prudently implemented new program does show signs of failure, a contingency plan should be available. Finally,

10

management must protect the prudent risk taker; if not, there will be no innovation.

- Change and innovation must become part of everyone's job. "If it's not invented here, it won't work" is a typical reaction to innovation. A good way to turn that attitude around is to involve the people who are going to use the innovation. But there is another, more substantive reason. The people who are directly involved in a process often can provide insight into how to improve it. They may not know exactly how, but they should be encouraged to point out opportunities and help work on solutions if that makes sense.

I remember talking to the new president of a well-established and well-known bank—call him "Don Green." Don had extensive experience in the industry, a good vision of what had to change, and was a good change manager. The bank had no audit or control problems, but was becoming less profitable in a vibrant market with a somewhat stable level of competition. After several months on the job Don said to me, "You know, it's awfully hard to change people who think they are doing the right thing." This was the crux of his challenge: The vast majority of the employees at all levels felt deep down they were doing the right thing.

Don spent an enormous amount of time in a player-coach mode. His first job was to get his constituency to realize change was required and not to feel threatened by it. You can't write a memo and change an institution overnight. He did many things, but one thing that seemed to help was focusing on a vision: Where would the customers and staff like to see the bank in five to ten years? The initial visions were not very different from where they presently were, but he got them to think about the changes that had occurred and tried to get them to project forward. This didn't get him very far until he introduced the staff gradually and informally to several people who were well respected as "futurists." This started the change process. Slowly the ideas started to percolate, and opportunities were identified. Where necessary, outside expertise was used, but in a well-defined, usually advisory, role. Don picked some relatively low-risk projects to start on, and he and the bank were on their way.

## PRINCIPLE 7: CULTURE CAN KILL

If you think managing innovation is hard, think about managing cultural change. Culture can be defined as a set of opinions, attitudes, and beliefs shared by a group of people. They affect what and how we communicate. But with communication there is at least the possibility that an opinion, attitude, or belief can be challenged and, perhaps over time, changed.

Culture affects more than communications. It affects the things we do or don't do. Let's take a hypothetical bank and profile its culture.

- Personal success is largely determined by effective role-playing.
- Senior management does not believe in managing by walking around, so most other managers don't either.
- Focusing on the customer and customer service are virtues talked about but not really practiced.
- Change is in truth strongly feared.
- Management believes its principal role is administering the business.
- There is a class/clan system in which interaction between various groups is not effective (e.g., tellers vs. platform people, operations people vs. sellers, vice presidents vs. non-vice presidents).
- The bank is a club and customers aren't members.

None of these things has been written down or discussed in the hypothetical bank, but they all exert a powerful influence on how it is managed on a day-to-day basis. In the changing environment consumer banking is in today, our hypothetical bank is doomed.

If we are aware of the danger, we can take two steps to avert it. One is diagnosing the bank's present culture and two is building a culture that is consistent with the bank's vision and mission.

Diagnosing a corporate culture may not be a science, but it does allow us to suggest some cultural values that should be in place and to recognize some tangible signs that they exist. For example, one important cultural value is that management's principal role is supporting the customer's interaction with the bank. A tangible sign of this value is management being present (on a regular basis) at the interaction. (Chapter 33 is devoted to diagnosing corporate culture.)

In terms of building the culture, there are two specific areas to concentrate on. The first is sales. We can determine what the profile of a sales culture should be and then work on growing that culture. The second is ensuring that we provide whatever personnel support we can to each employee. This not only helps them do a better job, but sends a message that they are important and we care. If management does not send that signal to the staff, the staff may not feel that customers are important.

Culture is the hardest thing we will have to manage, but knowing that it can kill will keep us on our toes.

Managing a consumer bank is a complex and changing affair. In a transactional environment we might unknowingly get off the critical path to success. The manager who understands the seven essential principles outlined in this chapter has a better chance of staying on track.

# CREATING A VISION

# Chapter 2

# How to Create
# a Vision

A vision is a word picture of how the bank wishes to be perceived by its constituents: customers, employees, and shareholders. It is something that could and should appear in the annual report. In fact, it's more important than this year's numbers because it affects the future numbers.

The first step in creating a vision is to set guidelines to help determine if the statement we develop is a vision.

- The vision statement must be capable of driving the business. It must suggest or state a test that can be used in guiding the management of the business.

- It must be shared by the constituency. They must understand it and agree with it.

- It must be simply stated. The simpler the better, not only in terms of understanding, but also in terms of using it in conversation with customers and staff, in written communication, in decision making, and other daily activities.

- It must be brief. This will make it easier to use, perhaps as part of a logo.

- It should be memorable. If the vision is insightful and well crafted, it probably will be remembered and applied.

- The vision should be broad enough to allow for growth of the business. If you create a new vision every year, you are going to spend an inordinate amount of time changing gears— probably with little payoff.

The operative word in the guidelines is *shared.* Whatever process we use, the end result will be shared by the constituents.

There are several ways to do this. The CEO can visit the mount and come back with a vision. This might make a good B movie but not a terribly useful vision. The CEO could more productively meet with a cross-section of the constituency to discuss the value of a vision and ask them to come up with several suggestions. If this process produces a vision that looks like a pale imitation of what the business is today, the CEO can suggest outside catalytic and creative help. Writing a vision is, after all, a skill.

After several visions have been developed, they can be used as a springboard for discussion. What does a particular vision mean in terms of next steps; is it a revolution or an evolution? How would we get to the state pictured in the vision? What are the associated risks? What are the rewards?

Once these questions are considered, the trade-offs between one vision and another should be more obvious. The CEO can then take the show on the road and see how it plays. In other words, the process of broadening and deepening the constituency can continue.

Guide 2 summarizes the main components of a vision statement and may be a useful guide in developing such a document. Once we have a vision that meets all the criteria we set, the next step is to make sure we use it. A vision can be used in one of three ways. It becomes a test we can use when allocating resources (i.e., is the resource essential to implement the vision?). It may imply a need for new skills, and it can be used to give each employee a charter to action.

It takes time and commitment to create a vision, but it is one of the seven essential principles for successful management of a consumer bank.

## GUIDE 2
## Creating a Vision Statement

*Definition:*   A word picture of how the bank wishes to be perceived by its constituents: customers, employees, and shareholders.

*Guidelines:*

- Drives the business
- Shared
- Simple
- Brief
- Memorable
- Broad enough to permit growth

*Example:*   We will differentiate ourselves by setting and maintaining the standards by which banking is judged. We will have met those standards when our customers think of us as their bank, when employees prefer to work for our bank, and when shareholders receive a superior return on their investment.

# Chapter 3

# Managing the Resources

In a regulated banking environment, the main variable that management had to worry about was expenses. The federal government more or less decided what the consumer needed, how much it should cost, and who (what type of institution) would meet the need. Management's challenge was to operate the bank as cheaply as possible; hence the focus on expense control.

This model does not work in a deregulated environment. Customers have choices and varying amounts of profit to bring to a bank. Managers still have expenses to worry about, but now the idea is to match the expenses with the potential revenue a customer could bring to the institution.

Let's take the case of a marginally profitable branch. Someone has suggested it be closed. The expenses that would be saved, after the closing expenses, would go right to the bottom line. At first blush, this appears to be the right thing to do, but let's ask a few questions: Is the branch an appropriate vehicle for achieving our vision of the bank? If it is, what would happen if we spent more money, not less? How would we spend it? Let's assume that we would spend it to enhance the human and physical resources of the branch, with the objective of getting more business from existing customers and attracting new customers. If we estimate the required incremental expenses and the incremental revenue, we might find that enhancing the bank would be attractive from an investment point of view.

Expenses, then, should be viewed as resources to achieve our vision and should be managed as an investment. How do we do that?

The first step is to review all current expenses and see if they will help achieve the vision. Is the expense designed to serve our target customer? Is the need the expense serves one that is identified in the vision statement? Expenses that don't pass this test are candidates for elimination.

The second step is to determine what level of expenses will permit us to most profitably satisfy the needs of our customers over time. We may find that by better understanding what the real needs are, we can meet them in a more profit effective fashion (for example, increasing the functionality of self-service systems). We may find that we are not spending enough money.

The third step is to view the expenses as investments and analyze how attractive they are. This involves estimating the profit potential of our target customers and what reasonable share of that potential we might capture. We may find we have some marginal investments.

We can follow the same general approach in analyzing proposed or new expenses. Make sure the following questions have been addressed:

- What customer need will this investment address?
- What is the value of satisfying that need to the customer?
- In what different ways could it be satisfied?
- What are the customer's priorities in selecting a solution?
- What are the various returns on the different solutions?
- How long will it take to start making money on the consumer?
- How difficult is the solution to achieve?

21

- Is the solution as simple as possible for the customer or staff to use?

- Are there any downtime or contingency issues?

If there is any one danger to watch for in managing expenses, it is separating expenses from the potential revenue of each customer. If you are managing expenses separately from revenue, you are not managing profit.

# DEVELOPING
## A STRATEGY

# Chapter 4

# SELECTING ONE OF
# FOUR CORE STRATEGIES

A 1987 consumer survey conducted by *American Banker* found that "If Americans could design their ideal bank, it would look nothing like what bankers are creating for themselves." Following are examples of how far apart consumer desires are from common bank strategies:

- Consumers want to do their banking with people; bankers want them to use machines.

- Consumers like to shop among multiple financial institutions; bankers want them to consolidate all their business in one place.

- Consumers like checks and cash; bankers want them to use plastic at the point of sale.

- Consumers want to buy mutual funds, stock, and insurance from specialists; bankers want to sell them those products.

- Consumers are divided about mixing banking and commerce; bankers are pushing for elimination of barriers to competition.

In order to be successful in the long run, strategies must meet the needs of both the banks and the consumers. This was not true in a regulated environment, where the consumer had little choice, but it is true in a deregulated environment. Financial services are a basic need, so in a competitive environment, the companies that profitably meet those needs will be the survivors. There are only four possible strategies for achieving this goal.

The two variables in these strategies are customers and needs. As Guide 3 depicts, we can target our business toward one or all customers, and toward satisfying some or all of their needs.

In deciding what quadrant we want to be in we must consider market opportunity, our bank's strengths and weaknesses, and the implications of being in a particular quadrant.

In order to avoid the problem the *American Banker* survey highlighted, we must think about the opportunities rigorously from both the customers' and the bank's point of view; customers have financial service needs, and the bank has profitability needs, so it becomes a question of identifying product offerings that do both. The ATM would be a classic example of this for some customers and some banks.

For each market we operate in we can start with a sense of what the financial needs are, what the existing and new ways to meet these needs are, and what the financial dynamics may be. Let's take an example: getting cash. This could be done in one of three ways: in a branch, via an ATM, or at the point of sale. Each

---

**GUIDE 3**
**Identifying the Four Core Strategies**

| Some Customers<br>All Needs | All Customers<br>All Needs |
|:---:|:---:|
| Some Customers<br>Some Needs | All Customers<br>Some Needs |

alternative has different implications for our bank, based on customer needs, preference, options, and our bank's share of the business. If we think there is a fourth alternative and have no useful data, we will need some market research. With knowledge of existing or new costs, we can assess the cost involved in meeting that need. Considerations include capital costs, operating expense, revenue, economies of scale, and rates of return.

This helps us understand what it would mean to offer this one service in one market to all customers. We might also consider what it would mean to offer this service only to a selected group of customers. We can do this for all the major financial needs of the consumers in our market. Based on the ownership patterns, share trends, and our costs, we can understand what it would mean to offer different groups of services. We also can determine if there are any groups of customers that are particularly attractive.

Before developing a strategy, we must identify the bank's strengths and weaknesses. To do so, consider the following issues:

- What is the bank's image in the marketplace?

- Does it have an established franchise among certain customers?

- Is there product expertise (for example, Merrill Lynch's CMA)?

- Is the bank's market share a potential problem or an opportunity?

- What expertise does the bank have that may be relevant to capitalizing on an opportunity (for example, technology)?

- What level of risk appears tolerable to the bank?

- Do the vision and mission suggest a clear commitment to certain opportunities?

- What level of capital and operating expenses might be reasonably committed to an opportunity?

- How successful have we been in innovation? Did we learn any lessons?

- How entrenched and formidable is the competition? Are there any available niches?

The best way to answer these questions may be to ask a cross-section of the bank to participate in a short, structured brainstorming session. Select the participants for their knowledge of the bank and ability to communicate. The result should be a specific list of the bank's strengths and weaknesses. Once we have this information, we can think about a strategy. The strategy we select will depend on what quadrant we are in.

## ALL CUSTOMERS/ALL NEEDS

A business that uses this strategy is probably the most complex to manage, given the multiplicity of customer needs, customer groups, and product offerings. The culture at such a bank is probably rich and varied, which in itself can be a complex issue to manage, even in a static environment; in a dynamic environment, managing innovation is a high-risk/high-reward business. We can look for guidance from Alexander Pope, who warned, "Be not the first by whom the new are tried, Nor yet the last to lay the old aside."

Being in this quadrant usually implies major capital commitment and may require a longer view of the business. The quarter by quarter approach won't permit sufficient lead time to see the fruits of the investments. Without profitability data on each customer, it becomes very easy in this quadrant to wind up subsidizing some customers.

Developing an approach to the customer that clearly says we want all of your business becomes crucial; product offerings should be priced to encourage customers to bring us all their business. Entrenched bureaucracy or red tape could mean that the customer who wanders through the door is never connected with all the resources the bank has invested in. From a communications point of view this strategy may be the simplest to implement because we are not dealing with subsets of customers and needs. The bank is committed to serving all the customers in its market.

## ALL CUSTOMERS/SOME NEEDS

By not serving all the needs of its customers, a bank can minimize the investment required and avoid entrenched head-on competition. With this strategy it is very important from both the customer's and the bank's point of view to communicate clearly what needs the bank satisfies. This may involve a superior track record in meeting those needs, expertise in the field, or innovation. Image and franchise can be very important. Stand-alone or unbundled pricing may be critical to profitability. Value or price may be the hot button in selling to the consumer.

## SOME CUSTOMERS/ALL NEEDS

Clarity in customer targeting is essential with this strategy. The bank in this quadrant will probably seek to identify with its customer group to facilitate communication, demonstrate commitment, and serve customers. Its expertise is in dealing with a specific type of customer, so staffing becomes critical both from a perception and performance point of view.

A long-term investment on the part of the bank may be required to identify it effectively with a particular group of customers. For example, a bank might sponsor an annual event that is closely associated with a certain group, such as retired people. The product offering should capture the essence of the targeted group. As an example, if a salient characteristic is that the group is asset rich and time poor, the products should individually and collectively play to that theme.

Identifying new customers may be a problem, particularly if the target customers and their financial needs are changing.

## SOME CUSTOMERS/SOME NEEDS

The market niche may be small with this strategy, which makes it easy to manage and differentiate. The risk is that the need for the niche may change dramatically or disappear. Hence management must be very plugged into the industry, quite adept at sensing change, and very focused on what their business is. This suggests a need to be a leader in the niche, setting the standards by which the industry is judged. Indeed, that may be the attraction for the customers. But whatever the attraction is, management must actively identify new customers. Stand-alone pricing is vital in both attracting and retaining customers.

The capital requirements for this strategy may be relatively small but creativity and innovation are vital.

Having identified market opportunities, outlined the strengths and weaknesses of the bank, and thought about the implications of being in one quadrant versus another, we should be able to articulate a strategy. The strategy statement will talk about a specific set of customers, their specific needs, and a proposed hot button. Some of the typical hot buttons may be quantity, value/price, innovation, expertise. An effective strategy statement might read as follows:

> Our strategy is to serve the transaction and investment needs of all the customers in our marketplace in a high value-to-price ratio.

The strategy statement will help us develop targeted plans that will deliver on the strategy. It will help us communicate with our staff, customers, and the general public, and it can ensure that all our efforts and resources are channeled in a direction that is consistent with the strategy statement.

Strategy statements can and sometimes should change over time, but we don't want to forget the Titanic principle: The larger the enterprise, the longer it takes to change course. So we must build into our thinking the amount of time required to change.

In developing one of these four basic strategies, it is important to have a complete understanding of consumers' needs and the opportunities available to the institution. Otherwise the opportunity to leverage the strengths and minimize the weaknesses of the bank will be missed. The implications of a particular strategy will not be fully dimensioned.

# Chapter 5

# ANALYZING THE MARKET

Market analysis is the basis for successful business management. There are three essential steps in this process: understanding the customers, defining their needs, and analyzing the opportunities.

## STEP 1: UNDERSTANDING CUSTOMERS

Factors such as age, income, education, occupation, marital status, and absence or presence of children in the home can reveal a lot about who the bank's customers are and how they behave vis-à-vis the financial service industry—what products or services they are likely to want, and their ability to pay for them. (See Guide 4 for a list of key demographics.)

What products does the customer "own" and what supplier is used for each service? Include as many services as the customer uses: transaction accounts, investment accounts, insurance, credit products, safe-deposits, travelers checks, ATMs, etc. How long has each product been owned?

Any information that helps paint a picture of current product and service behavior is useful. (See Guide 5 for a list of basic financial service products.)

In addition to knowing what specific services the customer "owns," we will want to know to what degree the services are used: How many times does the customer use the ATM, visit the branch, call on the telephone, mail in a request, or use a PC? Ranges are

---

**GUIDE 4**
**Key Demographics**

- Number of people in household
- Age of household members
- Marital status of household head
- Educational level of household head
- Occupation of head of household
- Number of full-time and part-time workers
- Ownership of residence
- Years at present residence
- Total household income
- County and zip code of residence

---

often used to ask this question. This information may suggest a preference in delivery systems or a specific need. (See Guide 6 for a list of basic transaction questions.)

Specific questions on pricing and fees can reveal how much profit a customer generates. Based on all the services the customer uses and the transaction patterns, we should be able to calculate the revenue the customer generates, the expenses directly incurred, any other related expenses, and the profit of the customer. The total profit generated lets us know how important the customer is, our current share, and what the incremental opportunity is for us to do business with that customer.

## GUIDE 5
## Basic Financial Service Products

- Checking account
- Money market account
- Savings account
- NOW account
- Savings club account
- CD
- Auto loan
- Personal loan
- Revolving credit line
- Bank credit card
- Mortgage
- Trust or estate service
- Investment advisory service
- Financial planning service
- Safe deposit box
- ATM service
- Telephone bill paying
- Debit card
- Direct deposit of social security, retirement income, pay, etc.
- IRA, KEOGH, or 401-K
- T+E cards
- Leased automobile
- Margin account
- Vested pension
- Specific types of insurance
- Full or discount brokerage service
- Stocks or bonds
- Mutual funds

---

**GUIDE 6**
**Basic Transactions**

- Number of ATM usages
- Names of financial institutions used
- Number and purpose of visits to financial institutions
- Name, number and purpose of visits to nontraditional financial institutions to conduct financial transactions (e.g., cashing a check at a supermarket)
- Number and purpose of financial transactions accomplished by telephone, mail, and PC
- Distance traveled to complete financial transaction
- Number of checks written, trades initiated, or other transactions

---

## STEP 2: DEFINING CUSTOMER NEEDS

Here we want as complete an inventory of the financial service needs of the customer as possible.

What needs does the customer currently have that are satisfied, and how well are they being satisfied? Some insight may be gained from the services they currently own or use and why they like or dislike particular features of the product. Transaction patterns can also be useful in understanding time and place convenience, preference for face-to-face banking, importance of security, contact, and other considerations. Demographic information may suggest needs such as education financing, retirement planning, emphasis on credit products early in life and deposit products later in life, or mortgage financing.

The number and type of financial service suppliers a customer uses may suggest a need to avoid risk, or a preference to buy certain products from certain suppliers, such as insurance from insurance agents, and traditional bank products from banks. It also may add information in terms of delivery preference (e.g., a customer uses mail predominantly with suppliers, or the suppliers are all near work). The fact that a customer cannot recall who the supplier is for a particular service might be significant.

While it may be possible to get some inferential data as we did above (particularly asking questions about product features), we probably have to ask other types of questions. We can ask consumers what additional "things" a bank or insurance company could do for them, but questions that explore how the consumer thinks about financial services might be more illuminating. Answers to these types of attitudinal questions stimulate the researcher and manager to start thinking like customers. (See Guide 7 for a list of attitudinal questions.)

In addition to gathering information about customer needs, we also have to understand how a customer trades off one need against another to arrive at a financial decision. For example, if the dominant needs are safety and rate, many decisions are already made. If lifestyle is an underlying major need, time and place convenience may be paramount. Financial institutions can impact and even create priorities, so the information gathered here must be tempered with opportunity available to the financial institutions. For example, place convenience can be made more important by an increase in number of branches and offices. Time convenience can be made more important by 24-hour ATMs.

A word about the data-gathering aspects of steps 1 and 2. The manner in which the data are gathered will affect the value of the data. How people are contacted, who is spoken to, precise wording of questions, sequencing of questions, skill of the interviewer, and testing of the questionnaire all affect the responses we receive. Fortunately, there are experts we can use in this field, including market researchers, consumer psychologists, and research analysts.

The value of gathering the data is summed up by Peters and Waterman in *In Search of Excellence*:

---

**GUIDE 7**
**Financial Attitudes**

What does the consumer think about:

- Insurance decisions
- Savings decisions
- Investment decisions
- Personal values
- Risk preferences
- Return on investment goals
- Attitudes toward money
- Lifestyle issues
- Control
- Privacy
- Communication styles

---

Show us a company without a good fact base—a good quantitative picture of its customers, markets and competitors—and we will show you one in which priorities are set with the most byzantine of political maneuvering.

## STEP 3: ANALYZING OPPORTUNITIES

At this point we want to look at the data collected in steps 1 and 2, any other market research, and ideas from senior management and start understanding the opportunity. There are four basic questions to ask:

- *What is the need?* Since our business is satisfying financial needs, we should be able to state what need we are trying to satisfy, how well it is currently satisfied, and how important the need is to the potential buyer.

- *How might we satisfy the need?* We can start with a list of things we would have to do. It may be linking together existing products or processes, or borrowing a product, process, or idea from another business, such as using a direct-mail catalogue to sell bank products. If it is fairly complex, we may break the process of satisfying the need into component pieces or a series of conditions that would have to be satisfied. There can be a long or short, easy or simple process. At some point in time it may be appropriate to consult with people who have expertise in creative problem solving and tailor a process to your needs.

- *What is the payoff?* If there is an identifiable need, and a reasonable way of satisfying the need, what is the payoff? What can we reasonably expect the customer to do, and how many customers over time might do it? Here is where the detailed product ownership and usage data (gathered in step 1) become very useful. By knowing who the product may be targeted at, what total profit these customers generate, and their past practices and trade-off decisions, we can estimate what our rewards may be over time.

- *What are the issues?* What additional crucial questions must be answered to be able to conclude that there is at least a hypothetical product that we can profitably offer?

The trick in doing this step well is balance. It is very easy to spend an enormous amount of time and money to find out if there is an opportunity. But, in fact, we are only looking for a sense that we should proceed. Once we have acquired the necessary data, we can start analyzing our investment opportunities.

# Chapter 6

# Segmenting the Market by Profit Potential

Identifying the common characteristics of a group of customers is one way to define cost-effective ways for reaching these customers. The question is, what are the characteristics that will be most helpful in managing our business—profitably satisfying customers' needs?

In 1963 and in 1983 the Federal Reserve Board sponsored studies, conducted by the Survey Research Center of the University of Michigan, that analyzed wealth in the United States. These studies were unique because they included an adequate sample of households in the upper net worth levels. Random surveys usually underrepresent these households.

The total net worth of American families in 1983 was $10.6 trillion, distributed as follows:

| | |
|---|---|
| Top ½ of 1% of all households | 35% |
| Second ½ of 1% of all households | 7% |
| 90–99% of all households | 30% |
| 0–90% of all households | 28% |

Thus, ½ of 1 percent of the households controlled 35 percent of the net worth at one end of the spectrum, and 90 percent of all households controlled 28 percent at the other end. Guide 8 indicates the number of households in each group, the group's range of wealth, and its average net worth. The average net worth for the top ½ of 1 percent was $8.9 million, versus $39,584 at the other end of the spectrum.

While we cannot equate net worth per household with financial service profit, the data suggest a concentration of profit potential in a relatively small percentage of households. This in fact is what a 1982 profitability study found, based on 5,700 households in seven states.

**GUIDE 8**
**Average Net Wealth Per Household, 1983**

|  | Number of Households | Range of Net Wealth Per Household | Average Wealth Per Household |
|---|---|---|---|
| Top 1/2 of 1% of Households | 419,590 | $2,509,750 and above | $8,851,736 |
| 2nd 1/2 of 1% of Households | 419,590 | $1,422,600– $2,509,749 | $1,702,376 |
| 90–99% of Households | 7,552,620 | $ 206,341– $1,422,599 | $ 419,616 |
| 0–90% of Households | 75,526,200 | $ 206,340 and below | $ 39,584 |

Source: *The Concentration of Wealth in the United States.* Published by The Joint Economic Committee, U.S. Congress, July 1986, p. 27.

35 percent of the total market generated negative 7 percent of profits (deficit segment).

45 percent of the total market generated 16 percent of profit (marginal segment).

20 percent of the total market generated 91 percent of net profit (high profit segment).

The bar chart in Guide 9 shows the net profit per household. The average net profit per household by segment was $256, but that number is meaningless in understanding the market, since 35 percent of the market generated a negative profit of − $48 and 20 percent of the market generated an average net profit of $1,185.

For planning purposes, then, some segmentation of the market based on profitability will be critical. Let's consider three groups of customers: low, medium, and high profit potential. What can we generally say about each group?

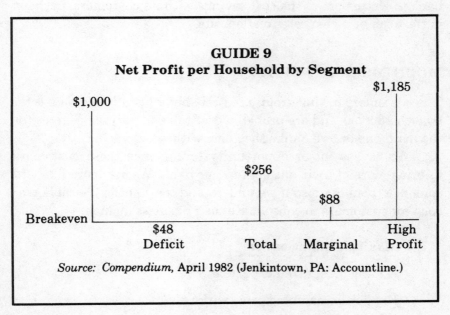

**GUIDE 9**
**Net Profit per Household by Segment**

Source: Compendium, April 1982 (Jenkintown, PA: Accountline.)

## LOW PROFIT GROUP

By definition, each of the households in this group has relatively low profit. Even modest changes in revenue spreads and expenses can cause some or all of this group to be unprofitable. This thin margin dynamic drains the business. Rate wars can make this market like the North Atlantic in winter. As suggested earlier, some of these customers may have a negative profit contribution to a bank.

Most of the customers in this group use more than one financial institution (as do customers in all groups), so in theory there is a potential for increased profits if the customers will bring all or most of their profit to our institution. But given the tendency of most customers not to consolidate all their business with one institution, this will not be an easy sell.

Net, the major business issue here is profitability, and the major opportunity is devising product offerings that are cheaper to deliver and still satisfy customers' needs. One possibility is for the bank to share part of the cost savings with its customers, perhaps in the form of higher rates on deposits.

## MEDIUM PROFIT GROUP

The customers in this group are probably all profitable on a total household basis and are probably profitable to varying degrees for the main one or two banks they deal with.

We have a major opportunity to convince these customers to bring more of their business to our bank. We are more likely to convince them to do so if we understand their needs. Possible reasons for customers to consolidate their business include:

- Making banking easier

- Adding recognized expertise

- Explicitly matching price with value

Profitability is by definition a function of product ownership and usage. Ownership is likely to increase if the sales staff is effective. Hence the importance of product knowledge and training. Relationship pricing becomes important where customers have a clear incentive to bring more of their business to one bank. Usage may increase with appropriate pricing, simplicity of access, and communicating new ways to use the product.

Because these customers have a greater profit potential than the low profit group, a different level of service—one that is perhaps more expensive—can be profit-effective if it meets their needs. Research is needed to identify what these needs are and what customers are willing to pay for.

## HIGH PROFIT GROUP

This group may be smaller than the others, so the economies of scale may not be present and, indeed, may not be necessary. But it is essential to understand how many of these customers are in our market, what our share of the households is, and their profit potential. These customers typically have a broad array of financial needs and use a broad array of products and suppliers. If they are our target market, we must plan to meet their needs. With these customers we have in theory the greatest flexibility in expenses to profitably meet their needs. Custom-tailoring of resources is possible, and probably essential.

Because there are so few of them, it is difficult to find and acquire high profit customers. Referrals can be an important and cost-effective source of new business. And, although these customers have significant profit potential, there may be a long lead time to close a sale.

In placing your own customers into the three profit groups, it may be helpful to prepare a matrix similar to the one in Guide 10. You may not agree with the specific low, medium, and high labels applied to each of the factors, but you will find that your market has three very different groups of customers in terms of

---

**GUIDE 10**
**Three Major Customer Groups**

|  | Low Profit | Medium Profit | High Profit |
|---|---|---|---|
| Profitability/ relationship | L | M | H |
| Rate of return | L | M | H |
| Competition | M | L | H |
| Image of any bank as main financial service supplier | H | M | L |
| Time to bond a relationship | L | M | H |
| Service level required | L | M | H |
| Staff competence/ knowledge required | L | H | M |
| Major business issue | Profitability | Consolidation | Marketing |

L = Low, M = Medium, H = High

---

profit potential. Each group reflects different business issues. For example, in the low profit group reducing expenses may be vital to increasing profit, while in the high profit group increasing expenses may be a viable way to boost profitability.

In summary, if there is a single message concerning customers it is that they are not alike from a profit point of view, and understanding these differences is critical to success. The danger is that we will use the concept of segmentation in managing our business but select a factor like age or income to differentiate one group from another. These factors may or may not relate directly to profitability. By using profitability directly as our point of difference, we can decide how best to satisfy our customers' needs and our shareholders.

# Chapter 7

# WRITING A SUCCESSFUL BUSINESS PLAN

"My salespeople don't have time to prepare business plans; they're too busy selling," said one manager at a company meeting. The same manager several months later said, "They don't have time to sell, they're too busy working on business plans." Someone else in the meeting said, "There is no reason for branch managers to prepare business plans. They know what they have to do, and they get enough instructions."

The irony of the conversation is that successful branch managers have a definite plan for managing their branch. They know there are certain things that have to be done, and they automatically go about doing them. Since they can't do everything themselves, they share their plan with the staff in a way that generates commitment. The plan is a tool for communicating, team building, and reaching objectives. The plan also makes the managers more effective in dealing with people outside the bank, their bosses, support people, and customers.

Often, the plan is not a lengthy, beautifully written document but rather an outline on a piece of paper for the manager's reference. Where necessary, pieces of the plan are carefully spelled out and discussed with the appropriate people. Who prepares the plan is critical. Peters and Waterman in *In Search of Excellence* (p. 31) quote Texas Instrument's Patrick Haggerty, who insisted that "those who *implement* the plans must *make* the plans."

What is a business plan? It's a collection of data, ideas, and specific actions designed to fulfill the mission of the person preparing it. This may be the branch manager, support manager, senior managers, or sales staff. A business plan gives the manager a way to:

- Think about, discuss, and get information out of data

- Share or find a direction

- Secure buy-in from the parties involved in executing the plan: the boss, the customer, the staff

- Think about events *before* they happen, to manage them most effectively

- Monitor progress towards an objective

- Ensure everyone is pulling in the same direction

Guide 11 is a sample business plan outline. Let's look at each element in the plan.


## INTRODUCTION

The introduction should do at least two things. It should establish the link between the branch and the larger business unit it is part of. This may be a playing back of the mission, vision, and strategy statement of the larger unit and relating it to the branch. The introduction should also give an overview of where the branch is at present. Has it just failed an audit? Won a sales contest? Experienced service problems? This can suggest an order in which things should be done.

The successful branch manager is keenly aware of the point that Richard Norman made in his book *Service Management* when he said, "A service organization is a complex and sensitive

---

**GUIDE 11**
**Branch Business Plan Outline**

- Introduction
  —tie to bank's mission, vision and strategy
  —frame broad issues
- Customers
- Competition
- Strategy
- Tactics
- Financials
- Issues
- Next Steps

---

*system.*"[1] So whatever the prevailing winds are from head office (service, sales, fees), he or she makes sure that the system is working. Focusing on rates, for instance, when the basics are not in place usually means that new customers will not be around very long.

## CUSTOMERS

Who are the customers the branch currently has?

- How many
- Profitability
- Geographic concentration
- Target group concentration

[1]Richard Norman, *Service Management* (New York: Wiley, 1984), p. 117.

What are their needs? The successful branch manager talks to the staff, the customers, and the general public in the area and has a good first-hand idea of what the needs are. There may be existing market research that helps. A branch manager who can't talk about the bank's customers isn't doing his or her job.

## COMPETITION

Who are the branch's competitors, and where are they located? Looking at customers' addresses, walking around the branch marketplace, and listening to customers should be a start. With this information, the manager can begin to understand what the competition is about, what they do well, what they emphasize, and whom they attract. The FDIC collects data on branches, so it may be possible to get a sense of the branch's market share and the current trends. Market share can be a function of how long the various branches were open, so it is helpful to know when the various branches in a neighborhood opened.

## STRATEGY

Based on the strategy of the larger business unit the manager belongs to and on the strength of the branch, its customers, and its competitors, the manager should be able to articulate a strategy. The strategy may be to focus on selected groups of customers and use truly differentiated levels of service to satisfy major customer needs at a profit. The strategy could also be price-driven or anything else that works. But whatever it is, it should be communicable in one simple sentence.

## TACTICS

What are the key action steps that must be undertaken to fix any problems in the branch and execute the strategy? These would relate to human resources, operations, MIS, sales, service, prospecting for new customers, and assistance from the support groups. They should be simply stated, relate to the strategy, and be actionable.

## FINANCIALS

While there are many financial measures that may be relevant to a particular branch, some of the more common are:

> *Growth.* Track and compare the last several years' growth with the future forecast. This includes number of relationships, accounts per relationship, total deposits, credit outstanding, fee income, expenses, and revenue.

> *Profitability.* How does growth translate into profitability? What has been the effect of interest rates? How successful has management been in managing fee income and expenses?

> *Efficiency.* If we were to compare the efficiency of this branch with other branches and with the industry over time, what would we conclude? Efficiency measures include profit per employee, profit per square foot of branch, and cost per dollar raised.

## ISSUES

What are the issues confronting the entrepreneurs operating this branch? Perhaps the market is changing, or the lease for the branch is up for renewal, or the branch is weak on service. The issues may not be easily or crisply addressed, but they are targeted as important.

## NEXT STEPS

Based on the situation, tactics, and issues, what are the next steps? Who's doing what, and in what time frame? This part of the plan is most useful in thinking about the action that must be

---

**GUIDE 12**
**Business Plan Checklist**

- Is it consistent with the vision, mission, and strategy of the business?

- Does the plan have a customer profitability focus?

- Are the issues clear?

- Is quantitative information crisply and concisely presented?

- Is there a clear set of objectives?

- Do the action plans tie to the objectives?

- Are the basics in place or about to be in place?

- What are the roles and opportunities?

- What constitutes success?

- What does the plan say about the staff and their roles and support?

---

taken and monitoring its progress. It becomes a road map and scorecard all in one.

Whether it is a branch manager's business plan or the business plan for a major bank, a balance must be struck between planning and doing. The amount of prose is not the concern. The concern is to address the relevant issues as if it were *our* money. The checklist in Guide 12 can be used to critique a business plan. As someone once said, "If you don't have a plan, you can plan on failing."

# Chapter 8

# GIVING EMPLOYEES A CHARTER FOR ACTION

Previous chapters have discussed how to develop a vision, mission, and strategy for a bank and how to manage resources as investments to achieve the vision. The next step is to stimulate the use of these resources by the contact staff. This is best done by carefully defining the responsibility and authority of each employee and then encouraging each to use the authority. We will discuss authority in this chapter and encouragement in subsequent chapters.

To underscore the importance of assigning responsibility, consider this situation: An account officer received word that the last cycle of money market statements had been printed and mailed with errors in the total balance. When the bank determined how it happened and what accounts were affected, a revised statement would be mailed out with an apology. Realizing that this could take ten days, the account officer suggested that they call their customers. The supervisor squelched the suggestion on the grounds that it would take too long, they didn't have all their telephone numbers, they didn't know who was affected or what to say. They had no authority to say anything.

As expected, a customer called this account officer, whom he had been dealing with for several years, and demanded to know what happened to the money in his money market account. Although the customer had made no significant withdrawals, there was $12,000 in there last month and less than $1,000 this month.

The customer wanted to close all his accounts with the bank immediately. This customer had been quite profitable to the bank over the years.

This wouldn't have happened if the bank's employees had a charter for action. Not a state or national charter to operate a bank, but a statement of the main principles that will guide the day-to-day operations of the bank—something to share with employees, customers, and stockholders (see Guide 13).

The charter statement should be constructed with the vision in mind and, like the vision, should be simply stated, concise, and memorable. It should embody the principles we believe in to guide our bank, and it should state them in a positive, active fashion. The charter statement should provide general guidance to all employees. One way to get the CEO to stand behind the charter statement is to prepare a draft and then seek the needed support and endorsement.

We can take this idea of a bank charter one step further and give each employee his or her own charter for action, as in Guide 14. It should be jointly developed by each employee and his or her supervisor, and it should make clear the employee's responsibilities and authority. Not only is this an efficient way of managing a service business, it also permits the contact person to act on behalf of the bank and as a partner in delivering services to the customer.

If we have done our homework carefully on these two charter ideas, we have set the stage for dramatic business growth. Most people want to do their job but just aren't certain how far they can go. Charters empower employees to utilize the bank's resources and the employees' own skills to their fullest extent. If we can unlock this wellspring, we are on the way to executing our mission.

The most likely obstacle to implementing this idea is risk aversion. There may be a reluctance to use two charters because some bankers like to tightly control employees. This problem usually suggests a much bigger problem, and that is culture. We will talk about culture in later chapters.

# GUIDE 13
## Charter Statement for the Bank

*Definition*   A charter defines the main principles that will guide the day-to-day operation of the business.

*Guidelines*

- Consistent with vision
- Simple
- Brief
- Memorable
- Broad enough to permit freedom of action
- Action-oriented

*Example*

- We are a service business.
- We make money by satisfying customers' financial needs.
- We will focus on the interaction between the customer and the bank.
- We will conduct the business with the understanding that the way the customer contact staff perceive the bank largely determines how the customer perceives the bank.
- We will structure the bank to bring decision makers as close as possible to the customers.
- We will focus the organization on profitably satisfying customers' needs and reward each staff member accordingly.
- We will conduct our business as efficiently, accurately, and simply as possible.

**GUIDE 14**
**Employee Charter**

Vision
— related to the bank's vision
— tailored to the unit that the employee works in

Mission
— again related to the bank's vision
— clearly stating the mission of the unit the employee works in

Charter
— authority
— responsibility

<u>   J. EMPLOYEE   </u>     <u>   G. SUPERVISOR   </u>

*DATE*

# INNOVATING
# FOR SURVIVAL

# Chapter 9

# MANAGING A
# WHIRLWIND OF CHANGE

One of my favorite stories, some would say apocryphal, is about the man who retired from a bank in the mid-seventies. He had spent more than 40 years in various branches of the bank and was managing its largest branch when he retired. At his retirement party someone asked him what was the biggest change he experienced in his career. Without hesitating, he said, "Airconditioning."

In a world where change had been infrequent and where the federal government made many of the decisions, it's reasonable to think that this could have happened, but the game has changed. Just how drastically we will explore in this chapter. Many changes have occurred, but we will highlight six:

- Deregulation

- Customer mix

- Customer knowledge

- Changing priorities

- Technology

- Management complexity

**Deregulation.** Deregulation of the financial services industry brings both challenges and opportunities. Let's compare the regulated banking industry with the deregulated.

*Consumer needs.* In a regulated industry, the government decides what the customer needs and lets banks meet those needs. With deregulation, banks can decide for themselves what needs they can best satisfy.

*Cost of raw material.* The raw material for banks is deposits. The interest rate that banks paid in a regulated environment was set by the government; in a deregulated environment banks can set their own interest rates based on costs to acquire, competition, and stability of sources of raw material.

*Price of goods sold.* The goods sold are loans and fees. Now banks can set their own interest rates based on their costs and customers' demand.

*Product restriction.* As deregulation proceeds, banks will be able to offer more products based on their customers' needs, the bank's image, franchise, costs, returns, time to sell the customer, and competition.

*Geographic restrictions.* Deregulation also is giving banks an opportunity for geographic expansion. Before proceeding, the banker must analyze the opportunity, the associated rates, the returns, and, most importantly, how fast to grow.

*Barriers to entry.* As barriers to entry are removed, banks face increased competition from other companies that serve the consumer and from entrepreneurs who know the service business or sense an investment opportunity.

**Customer Mix.** Many factors are operating here. More people work at home, the population is living longer, and the baby boomers are reaching their peak earning years. One model suggests that we first understand who our customers are, then understand their needs, and finally determine how best to serve them. Understanding how customers and non-customers have changed is critical to profitably meeting their needs. Census Bureau publications can be a good point to start researching one's market.

**Customer Knowledge.** Competition is a process that highlights differences between products or services. In doing so it can help the customer make more knowledgeable decisions. Anyone who has been in the branches for 20 years would agree that customers have become more knowledgeable. This trend will continue, and it will drive another industry—the information industry for consumers.

**Changing Priorities.** As customers and products change, and the information available changes, customers will reevaluate their priorities. Several years ago, customers may have searched for the closest branch. Today the issue may be 24-hour access or home banking privileges. The contact staff probably picks up insights into changing consumer priorities.

**Technology.** As school systems rely more and more on technology such as PCs to educate the students, the percentage of customers who are comfortable with technology will grow. This is both an opportunity and a challenge to a bank. The opportunity is to use it to meet the needs of the customer in a profit-effective fashion. The challenge is to make sure that the customer doesn't get lost, or that feedback and sales opportunities aren't missed.

**Management Complexity.** If the only change that had taken place was deregulation, this alone would have made the management of a consumer bank infinitely more complex. But when we add all the other changes into the equation, the result is that the consumer banking business today bears no resemblance to what it was 20 years ago. Having the same old players and playing by the same old rules is a way to lose the game.

Change cries for leadership. We sometimes make the mistake of thinking that leadership exists only at the top of an organization. It is needed there to form the social fabric of the organization and to mold the vision of the bank, but leadership can and should exist throughout the bank. The contact manager must be a leader as well as a support manager and a developer of new ideas. The authors of one recent book on leadership observe that "leadership is not so much the exercise of power itself as the empowerment of others."[1] Anyone who manages people can, with the right support, be a leader if he or she wants to lead.

What is a leader and what do they do?

"A leader is the kind of person to go tiger hunting with in the dark, because you are always sure they are there . . ."[2]

"The ability to organize all the forces that are in an enterprise and make them serve a common purpose"[3]

"The new leader is a listener, communicator, educator—an emotionally expressive and inspiring person who can create the right atmosphere, rather than make all the decisions himself."[4]

We can nurture leadership, and we can start by giving people the tools or the systems they need to run the business. Senior management can develop a culture that grows leaders. But when we have done all that, the person himself must possess a quality, and probably Carlzon's notion of emotional energy is most insightful. Leaders do not exist in theory, they exist in practice. The leader builds a winning team, and winning is part of being a leader.

[1]Warren Bennis and Burt Nanus, *Leaders: The Strategy for Taking Charge* (New York: Harper & Row, 1985), p. 225.

[2]*Of Interest to Executives* (Royal Bank of Canada, 1955), p. 25.

[3]Harwood F. Merrill, *Classics in Management* (AMA, 1970), p. 300.

[4]Jan Carlzon, *Moments of Truth* (Ballinger, 1987), p. 36.

# Chapter 10

# MAKING INNOVATION EVERYONE'S JOB

Innovation from the customer's point of view may be opening a branch a half hour earlier or introducing ATMs; innovation is simply a better way of meeting the customers' needs. In an environment that is undergoing massive changes—including customers' needs—innovation is necessary for survival. But unless the culture of the bank says that innovation is important, it won't happen.

The first task is to answer the question, "What does the culture say about innovation?" If the culture approves, we won't even have to ask. We will see innovation in action. If the culture is not receptive to change, we may get one of two responses to the question.

The first is that it's "too expensive." With this response we can at least identify an innovative idea with minimal risk and cost, implement it, and then measure the results. This incremental approach helps build a commitment to innovation in the culture. Introducing new people into the culture who believe in innovation is another approach.

The second response is that it's "not needed." This is harder to deal with because it may represent a mind-set. In this case we need to create an awareness of change that may drive a need for innovation. We also might try to sell an innovation as a cost reduction. This may not be possible in all cases, but innovation often leads to reduced cost; focus on that fact and downplay the innovative aspects.

Let's assume that we have solved the cultural problem or a least neutralized it. Now we can set about innovating. First focus on the customers and understand how their needs are changing or could be made to change. In fact, there are four preconditions to innovation.

*Listening to the customer.* Every time the customer interfaces with the bank we should be listening. In some cases we may not even have to ask a question; the customer might volunteer some information. All we have to do is listen. But listening is an acquired skill. Thinking about what we are going to say next often gets in the way of listening.

*Thinking about how to better meet customers' needs.* There is a natural opportunity to do this when the contact staff and supervisors meet to review their customers. While discussing each customer, the supervisor can ask how they might better meet the customer's needs. The ideas that emerge might relate to only one customer or to many customers. Indeed, they may not be solutions, but merely ideas for solutions or insights into opportunities.

*Supporting the change process.* Listening and thinking is supportive, but we may be able to do more, by being a catalyst for change. We can encourage an exchange of ideas between the contact staff and the support staff or outside experts on innovation. We can also experiment a bit by taking an idea and trying to implement it. But saying no to an idea is not supportive; we should see if we can improve it or suggest another one to think about.

*A commitment to change.* Just as being in the service business requires a commitment to service, being in a rapidly changing environment requires a commitment to change—to survive. Commitment can take the form of allocating resources for innovation and encouraging prudent risk taking.

With the four preconditions to innovation in place, we can think about how we might implement a change. Guide 15 illustrates one way to think about this process.

The first step in implementing change is to gather ideas from customers, staff, and outside sources. We are looking for an unsatisfied need or opportunity and some of the components of the solution. We are looking for pieces of a puzzle here, and intuition may play a role.

---

### GUIDE 15
### A Schematic for Managing Innovation

| Step | Action | Need |
| --- | --- | --- |
| 1. Ideas | Seeing a solution that isn't there— an unsatisfied customer need | Customer and staff input |
| 2. Linkage | Combining basic idea with business opportunity—a need of the bank | Vision, strategy |
| 3. Execution | Figure out how: (1)attention to detail, and (2) getting around problems | Form team |
| 4. Value Created | Measure results | Customer input |

---

The second step is linkage. Can we take the unsatisfied customer need and relate it to a need the bank has? This may simply be a need for profit or a need to fulfill a vision for the bank. It could be related to specific customers, specific products, or specific strengths of the bank. If we can establish the linkage, we may have the components of a win.

The third step is execution. All steps may occur with significant time gaps between them. For example, the technology may not be present today to execute our idea, but it might be next year. Our job in execution is to figure out how. A useful personal trait here is the ability to see obstacles as things to be gotten around, not stopped at. Attention to detail is vital, and the innovator must have the need to accomplish. These divergent personal traits suggest the need to involve a variety of people in executing the plan.

The fourth step is to confirm that value was really created, from both the customer's and the bank's point of view. Here again, we have to allow enough time to truly measure the return on our investment. This final step is also an opportunity to review why we were successful or unsuccessful in this particular instance and to see if there are any lessons for the future.

One of the lessons we will probably learn is that many people are involved in successful innovations, and making innovation everyone's job ensures that this process works well. One common problem here is that the people who will use, sell, or explain the innovation are themselves not sold on the idea. Several years ago, the head of a consumer bank decided that ATMs were the wave of the future and installed several in his branches at considerable expense and customer/staff inconvenience. In time, someone at head office noticed that the machines were not being used much. The reason was pretty straightforward: The contact staff were not convinced they were a good idea, so they did not try to convince the customers they were a good idea. Innovation must be focused towards the customers, and the contact staff must be behind it.

# Chapter 11

# Identifying
# New Customers

The marketing department has been very busy working on a marketing program to identify new customers. The idea seems to have originated with senior management, but no one knows for sure. In any event, marketing is developing a presentation for senior management describing an idea, demonstrating its synergy with the overall strategy, and suggesting the process continue. The ad agency becomes involved and the result is a fairly elaborate treatment of how the idea could be packaged. Marketing gets the go-ahead and the creative money it wants. After two more presentations to management, the product is introduced with a lot of fanfare. Three weeks later, no one wants to talk about it. It didn't do very well.

What went wrong, or what opportunities were not realized? What are the issues to be sensitive to next time around? The short answer is that they didn't understand the needs of the customers they were targeting or their willingness to buy. We can avoid that problem by thoroughly analyzing our market. As discussed in Chapter 5, this means understanding your customers, defining their needs, and analyzing the opportunities.

Let's assume we have done that and now are ready to develop an offering, prepare a business proposition, and then execute the plan. It's a three-step process.

**Step 1.** Assuming that there is an opportunity, we must determine how best to meet it. It may take many iterations, but the result should be a comprehensive but easily understood description of the offering from the *customer's* point of view. It may be helpful to describe the offering in terms of four key components.

*Menu.*   A simple description of the products, answering the question, What is this product? How does it work? What are its benefits for the customer and the bank? What needs does it satisfy? What choices does the customer have with this product? It should be the way you would design a menu in a restaurant.

*Price.*   How much does it cost? Are there different price levels for different options? Are there costs that apply only in certain circumstances, like late fees? Is there a different price if you have, or will buy, several different products? Net, what will it cost for a particular customer?

*Delivery.*   How is the product delivered? Does the customer go to the branch, can it be done over the telephone, by mail, on a PC? Does the customer have a choice? Does the choice of delivery affect price?

*Service.*   Is the offering self-service or full service? Who does the customer contact? Are there different people to contact for different things: renewal, errors, questions, advice, claims, redemptions? How much service are you buying?

After the offering description is written, we can use a schematic like the one in Guide 16 to critique and sharpen the description. The idea here is that if we put today's dollars into an opportunity, various factors (the holes in the funnel) impact our result in tomorrow's dollars. At the end of this step we should have a well-defined offering statement in which potential customers have expressed some interest.

**Step 2.** With the information we now have, we can put together a business proposition. The purpose here is to provide a

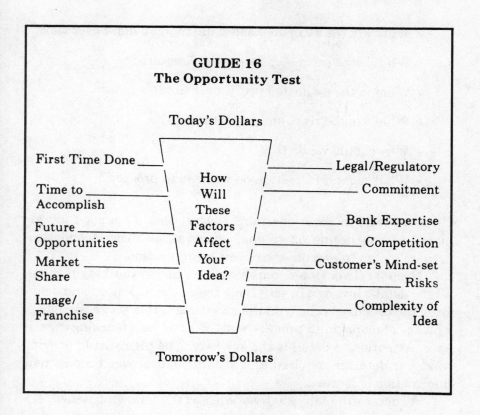

**GUIDE 16**
**The Opportunity Test**

Today's Dollars

First Time Done ____

Time to ____
Accomplish

Future ____
Opportunities

Market ____
Share

Image/ ____
Franchise

How Will These Factors Affect Your Idea?

____ Legal/Regulatory

____ Commitment

____ Bank Expertise

____ Competition

____ Customer's Mind-set

____ Risks

____ Complexity of Idea

Tomorrow's Dollars

clear answer to one question: Is this new product an investment we want to make, and why? In addition to profit considerations, it may be a defensive measure, an opportunity to differentiate our product line, an investment in the future, a piece of an overall marketing strategy.

We want our business proposition to address the following questions:

- Who is the target customer?

- What is the specific need to be addressed?

- What is the proposed offering?

- How might we sell it?

- What are the estimated sales and market share over time?

- What is the estimated investment required?

- What is the estimated profit over time?

- What are the risks and opportunities?

- Why should we do this?

- What more information do we need to proceed?

If the answers to these questions suggest that it's a good investment, we can decide on timing, approval, and issues and then prepare a plan to execute the business proposition.

**Step 3.** This step is partly an exercise in thinking through all the details involved in satisfying the customers' need and delivering the promised return on the investment. It is also a road map, a means of managing a process, and the basis for a learning experience. Attention to detail is the key here. The plan should provide whatever detail is required and should change over time as new information is learned.

A successful plan usually addresses the following issues:

- Marketing plan
  What is the hot button that will cause customers to buy the product?
  How can we best communicate the new offering to accomplish the sale?
  What detailed sales process will we follow?
  Is there to be a promotion of the new product?
  What pieces of communication material will be used (letters, signs, posters, brochures, sales aids)?
  What is the fulfillment process?
  What additional research is required?

- Training plan
  Who will be trained?
  What will they be trained to do?
  What training material is needed?
  Where can we go with questions?
  Who will test the training program?

- Support plan
  What is required?
  Who will do it?
  How will it work?
  What are the interrelationships?
  Who is responsible for what?
  Whom can we call with problems or suggestions?

- Communications plan to staff and customers
  What methods will be used to sell, inform and collect feedback from staff and customers?

- Goals
  What do we expect this plan to accomplish? Spell out in detail, down to the customer contact person.

- Incentive plan for the staff

- Management information systems that will be in place
  Samples
  What types?
  Who gets them?
  When?

- A detailed list of tasks with dates and responsibilities

- Program evaluation plan with staff and customer feedback

- Contingency plan if certain things fail to happen or the unexpected happens

---

**GUIDE 17**
**Project Management Checklist**

- Is the objective clearly and, if possible, quantitatively analyzed?
- Is the system that would achieve the objective spelled out in detail?
- Have all the tasks been documented with responsibilities and due dates?
- Is there a regular review of progress?
- Have contingency plans been developed?
- Has the system been tested before it is used?
- Is there a monitoring and feedback system in place?
- What lessons were learned?

---

Recalling Principle One from our first chapter, systems have interrelated parts and so do banks. To ensure that all the pieces of the system are working together we need good overall project management and a systematic management of details. Details are not for the other guy, they are for the person who wants to be successful. See Guide 17 for a project management checklist.

# Chapter 12

# DEVELOPING PRODUCTS THAT SELL

The CEO of one bank went to Washington to testify before a congressional committee; one of the committee members asked him how profitable his current customers were. The CEO said he really didn't know, but last time they checked (about a year ago), 60 percent of their customers were profitable. The questioner then asked which products the bank loses money on, but the CEO said that was hard to answer. Finally the congressman said, "I don't understand how you run your business!" Neither do I. Let's ask three questions about product profitability. First, we want to identify what products we lose money on. Second, we need to know how well the products satisfy our customers' needs. Third, identify opportunities to improve need satisfaction and profit.

We want to be able to calculate the profitability of each product we sell. Depending on usage and balance levels, a product could be profitable for one customer and not for another. Hence we will calculate the product profitability for each customer. We will wind up with a frequency distribution for each product that indicates how much money we make or lose. For example, we will be able to say that we make money on 95 percent of all checking accounts we currently sell, or we lose money on 75 percent of the safe-deposit boxes we rent.

After we have the frequency distribution for each product, we can make a preliminary determination of what products are not profitable and would require major changes to be profitable. We probably don't want to develop or continue marketing these products. As we proceed to analyze all our products from a customer need perspective, we will pay particular attention to these and determine whether we should drastically change them or discontinue them.

Let's assume we have red-flagged the unprofitable products and now seek feedback from our customers on how well current products are meeting their needs. We can analyze what product offerings we have specific feedback on, how many people have commented on a specific product offering, and in what degree of detail. We can prepare a summary of the customers' feedback and do two things with it. We can play it back to the contact staff with a questionnaire that solicits their feedback on how well our products meet certain needs, and we can identify the products and issues that need more specific feedback. Let's prioritize our search for more specific feedback based on a product's impact on bank profitability. We want to go after the big opportunities first.

A consumer banking market research professional can help get specific input on need satisfaction for those product offerings where this information would be of some value. The test here is if we had it, how valuable would it be vis-a-vis the cost of procuring the data.

At this point we should know the profitability of each product and have some sense of how well the product satisfies our customers' needs. We now have the data we need to decide what products we should enhance, what products we should drop, and what products we do not offer that we should. The decision should be based in part on what share of the customers' revenue in our market can we reasonably expect to get. If a product fits with the vision, mission, and strategy of the bank, fine, but if it does not, we should have a powerful reason to continue offering it (e.g., they are very profitable and perhaps can be spun off as a separate business). We will have picked up some of this information as we analyze our market (see Chapter 5).

If after analyzing the data you still cannot conceptualize a new or improved product offering where you sense there is a need, think about where the consumers in your market are in their life cycle and think about the various financial needs that arise as we go through life. For example, there may be a greater need for credit early in life and a greater need for deposit products later in life. Sorting the data by life cycle might suggest new or enhanced products. If all else fails, you may wish to seek the advice of professionals involved in developing new products.

When we have conceptualized a new product offering, we should be able to answer the following new product questions:

- Is the offering simple to explain?

- Is the offering easy to understand?

- Is it easy to use?

- Is it consistent?

- Is it competitive?

- What might the competitive reaction be?

- Is it believable?

- Does it require any special equipment or training?

- What is the estimated revenue and development expense?

At this point, if the investment opportunity appears attractive, we should pursue it. The bottom line is that the product must meet a need and be profitable. The CEO in our opening story hadn't forced that closure.

# Chapter 13

# DESIGNING PROFITABLE DELIVERY SYSTEMS

If we are to effectively analyze our current delivery system and recommend changes, we need to know specific information about the current usage of the delivery system and about the target customers' delivery preferences.

Let's use as an example a bank with no delivery systems other than one ATM. We could determine what customers used the machine, for what purposes, when. We could calculate the profitability of each customer and find out whether the bank makes money or loses money on the ATM. Further analysis may permit us to understand why we lose money because we don't have sufficient customers using the ATM or the revenue per customer appears to be low. Alternatively, we may have made money and further analysis may indicate that it is frequently used by our customer base. We would conduct some research and determine what the customers' delivery preferences are. Based on further analysis, we could determine what enhancements we can profitably make. Net, our one ATM bank could be managed with a relatively complete understanding of the profit dynamics of the business.

But if the delivery system in a bank involves more than ATMs, we might not have the data we need to analyze the overall system. This is a problem that won't go away. Increased real estate costs and operating expenses, coupled with competition that is offering a wide array of delivery systems, are eroding profit margins. On the other hand, consumers may continue to prefer branches with people in them. Without the data, it would be difficult to manage the business. How would we know if the branch was unprofitable? Assume that we know what delivery system each customer uses, how frequently, and for what purpose. We may wish to seek professional advice on how best to gather the information on a regular basis.

With this information and the vision, mission, and strategy, we can analyze current delivery systems and see how they support our plans. Understanding the profit dynamics of our target customers should help us determine what types of delivery systems they can afford. Understanding the needs we plan to serve and how we plan to serve them (e.g., low cost vs. high touch) may also help suggest certain types of delivery systems. At this point we can prepare a tentative action plan for the current delivery systems. What we need now is input from the customers. Let's take two different cases that we can explore with them.

In the first case, let's assume that the target customers are in the low profit group, as discussed in Chapter 6. The product offering we will be soliciting their reaction to would describe the menu of products (probably limited); the prices, interest paid on deposits, interest charged on loans, usage fees, etc.; delivery systems options (presumably a less expensive delivery system); and the service that would be available. It may be possible to price this product offering quite attractively, given the relatively low operating expenses. The test is, does it profitably satisfy the customers' needs? If the bank doesn't make money, there will be little incentive over time to serve this market; if the customers' needs are not met, they will look elsewhere. What may emerge is one or more self-service delivery systems coupled with a capability to discuss relationship products face to face with customers.

In the second case, let's assume that we are targeting the high profit customer. The products on the menu would probably be more extensive or more complex to deliver. The prices might be more expensive than in the lost cost case. There could be a flat fee for the service in addition to interest charges on loans or interest paid for deposits. The delivery systems and the service could also be more costly because of the expertise or one-on-one nature of the customer contact.

In fact, the present branch may not be appropriate for either of the two cases we just described. It may be too expensive in the first case and too transactional in the second. Hence, in researching delivery systems, whatever they may be, we want to ensure that they are designed to meet customers' needs and generate a profit for the bank. Information on how customers make trade-offs is critical. Certain customers may pay a premium for ease of access to their bank, while others will always look for the best price. Understanding this trade-off phenomenon becomes critical as we design and test our product offerings.

The delivery system in the last analysis is a crucial component of how we execute a mission. The opportunity is to match customers' needs with delivery systems they can afford.

# FOCUSING ON THE REVENUE PROVIDER

# Chapter 14

# THE BUSINESS STARTS
# WITH THE CUSTOMER

Most people would agree that if they owned a business, they would focus on the source of revenue; they would have no need to incur expenses if they had no revenue. Well, we all are owners—owners in a bank. If we don't feel that ownership, we probably won't be making the right decisions.

Why do some banks focus on expenses rather than revenue? The president of a bank issued a memo about the next year's direction as a way of initiating the budget process. It was about six pages long, and one phrase in it said "expenses will increase X percent next year." That was the whole message of the memo. Managers could do pretty much as they liked, as long as it didn't cause expenses to go up more than that amount. Revenue wasn't even mentioned, other than to say it should "grow" in selected businesses.

In point of fact,

- The bank paid no attention to market share; its was decreasing.

- The culture rewarded people who had good control skills.

- The bank really wasn't committed to the consumer business.

The philosophy behind the memo was that expenses are for sure, revenue is a promise, and risk avoiders go for the sure thing. If you think this sounds like a recipe for going out of business, you're right.

How do we focus on the revenue provider? The first step, which we have already talked about, is to calculate the individual profitability of each customer. The second step is to relate our business decisions to the current and potential profitability of our customers.

There is another thing we can do. Each year when we prepare a budget for the next year, we can make sure that we start the process with input from the consumer. Not what management *thinks* the consumer thinks, but what the consumer really thinks. Let's frame a series of questions for our customers.

1. What did you like and dislike about what we did last year?

2. What would you like us to focus on next year?

   *Both of these questions should be asked pretty much as written. We are trying to get at what seems to be important to them without any prompting.*

3. How do you plan on changing your relationship with the bank next year?

   *If there seems to be some hesitation here, follow up with questions about changing their ownership and use of our product offering.*

4. How would you like the bank to change its allocation of resources?

   *If this gets no response, suggest specific resources, e.g., dollars, people, programs, or markets.*

5. How would you ideally like to interface with the bank?

   *If the response is "pretty much the way I currently do," ask respondents to describe how they presently interact with the bank. If they express some need to change but can't describe how they would like to change, ask their reaction to specific means of interacting—with or without people, with or without branches, with or without machines. Also where they would like to interact: home, office, or work.*

6. When you need someone to interface with, what type of person do you prefer?

   *We are looking for actionable descriptions, e.g., more knowledgeable about X, more authority, easier to access, a more confidential surrounding.*

7. How would you characterize the relationship you would like with the bank?

   *Possible answers include: as a transaction point, a source of advice, a relationship manager, information about my choices.*

8. What products would you then like your bank to provide?

   *Get their reactions to the major types of products the bank could provide. They may mention products the bank already provides.*

9. How would you like to pay for this product?

   *In addition to balances or fees, see how interested they are in a bundled or relationship pricing scheme.*

10. Would you recommend your bank to a friend? Why or why not?

    *There is a whole range of answers possible here, but the point is to identify things that would cause a referral.*

11. What percentage of your business would you like to give the bank?

    *If we were their ideal bank, what could we expect the customers to do?*

We probably will want assistance from a researcher skilled in getting representative data on the entire customer base. In packaging the results of the survey, make it as brief, simple, and actionable as possible. We now have input from the revenue suppliers that we can use to evaluate how profitably we can do these things.

This information can have many values. One is simply to factor the revenue provider into the planning process—to close the gap between what the customer wants and what the bank needs. It may disclose specific activities that the bank should change, expand, or eliminate. A second and more subtle value is that it can indicate the tone of the bank's interaction with the consumer. Perhaps there are unspoken opinions, attitudes, and beliefs that have to be changed. This cultural feedback can be a useful, but perhaps painful process.

We would like to see each employee put him or herself in the customer's shoes before acting. Managers at all levels can encourage this practice by doing it themselves.

# Chapter 15

# THE SERVICE
# PARTNERSHIP

Service is a partnership between the customer and the bank. Both parties actively participate in the interaction we call service. Someone does the serving and someone gets served. The one who does the serving is the junior partner in the deal and has to be comfortable with that role. If we personally aren't comfortable with that role, all the service strategies in the world will have little effect because service is fundamentally an attitude.

To understand what it means to provide a service, think of instances where you as a consumer received good service (from a restaurant, airline, hotel, bank, etc.) and write down how you felt about each experience. Now do the same for instances where you received poor service. Then try to identify what made the difference.

You will discover that there are three preconditions for the development of a service culture. If the preconditions are not met, spending money on service is a poor investment.

## PRECONDITION NO. 1: IS THERE A RECOGNIZED CUSTOMER?

On your two lists of service situations, were there instances where you did not seem to be central to what was going on? A process was occurring, but you were irrelevant. For example, you asked your bank to investigate a deposit you made that wasn't posted to your account. Whether it was a dollar or a million dollars, and whether you were a customer or a *very* profitable customer, you sense that the process would have been the same. In fact the process was the focus.

The culture has to recognize that there are customers. Process is not a customer.

## PRECONDITION NO. 2: WHO IS THE CUSTOMER?

Who has to be pleased—regulatory authorities, the board of directors, outside counsel, or management? If that question is not answered by "the customer," you are not in the service business. On your lists did you note any self-service experiences that were not user-friendly or confidential? Perhaps everyone's advice, except the revenue provider, was taken into consideration when these services were designed.

## PRECONDITION NO. 3: WHAT ARE THEIR NEEDS?

We want to make sure that the customers' basic common needs are identified and that they can choose how best to meet them. As a customer you may have been in a branch that was recently renovated, but when you asked staff in the branch for information they didn't know. Perhaps the money could have been better spent improving the knowledge level of the staff. Management had decided what the customer needed.

What can we do to make sure that these three preconditions are in place? We can build a commitment to service, and here is how to do that.

- The contact staff must have the tools to serve the customer —operating support, information about the customers and products, applications and brochures. If the contact staff receives second-class tools, the customers will probably receive second-class service.

- Housekeeping must be important. A branch that looks messy sends the message "We don't care."

- Management must be committed to defining what service means to the customer, monitoring it, and making whatever changes are needed to permit the bank to execute its mission.

- The various roles in the bank must be very clear, especially the notion that management supports the contact staff.

- The culture can say that service is important by rewarding those who provide good service.

Once these five tangible service commitments are made, we can look to the less tangible signs, which are the more important ones.

- How does the staff talk about customers? If with a gleam in their eye and pride in their heart, the attitudinal dimension of service—which is the essence of service—is in place.

- Does senior management personally become involved in service, like talking to customers or being their contact officer? The service entrepreneur wants to talk to his customers.

- Are the little things in place that say service is important— a smile, addressing people by their names, going out of your way to help someone?

If we have all these factors going for us, we probably are committed to service, and tactical programs to improve service will probably be successful. But there is at least one more thing we can do, and that is reinforce the central role of the contact staff. While the contact staff is the junior partner in the service partnership with the customer, we want to make sure that within the bank the message is clear that they are the regulators of profitability, and hence the stars. How do we do that?

- Acknowledge that the way you treat the contact staff is the way the customers will be treated.
- Give them recognition.
- Structure a reward system that says their results are important.
- Solicit their input and act upon it.
- Support them with dollars and example.
- Act as if they were the bank to their customers.
- Promote them if that makes sense and it's what they want.

While service may be hard to achieve, it's easy to lose, so, as we manage by walking around (discussed in *In Search of Excellence*), we must be attentive to the opportunities to be of service and learn about the business first hand.

There are endless dangers associated with managing service. One is that someone decides it's a staff job. This is an impossibility: Service must be the responsibility of those who are partners in its creation.

# Chapter 16

# Managing Customer Perceptions

Every time a customer interacts with the bank, there is an opportunity for the bank to impact the customer's perception of the bank, favorably, unfavorably, or not at all. Customer perceptions can be managed most effectively by setting up an ongoing employee communication program and paying attention to the basics that define a branch.

## EMPLOYEE COMMUNICATIONS

Bank customers interact with a wide range of staff members; unless these contact people are kept well informed by bank management, they can only interact with customers in the way they think management would prefer. Keeping the staff well informed requires hard work, but it is crucial to success in the service business.

The first prerequisite for successful employee communication is that the staff must understand the mission, vision, and strategy of the bank. This gives them a framework when they talk to customers. If a customer starts a conversation about a major new program of the bank, a teller can make a brief relevant comment instead of saying, "I don't know anything about that." Along these same lines, each staff member also must understand his or her charter. What issues, questions, comments, and suggestions can the staff member respond to without consulting with someone else? One valuable customer decided that she would no longer do business with a particular bank because she could never speak to any decision makers there. This would not have happened if employees understood the scope of their authority *and* the overall mission of the bank. Finally, on an ongoing basis, the staff must receive prompt day-to-day news about the bank, its plans, and its progress before the customers receive it.

If these three conditions are met, the contact staff will have enough knowledge to affect customer perceptions in a positive way.

In terms of day-to-day communication, the staff should know *who* they can ask for information. Perhaps it's their boss, perhaps it's someone who has product management responsibility, someone in operations, or someone in public affairs. The information should be timely, although this can become a process problem if many people must review what is sent out. The new chairman of AT&T solved that problem in one instance by writing his own speech and asking for comments. It was faster than having a committee write and agree on what he should say. While there may be legal or other reasons why something has to be said in a particular fashion, remember that the idea of communication is to convey a thought. This means that reports and memos should be clear, concise, and candid. If you have to read a staff memo five times to understand it, there's a problem. Candor in communications is easy to talk about but sometimes hard to achieve, as evidenced by one bank that reshuffled its senior management staff. The same day the changes were announced, a long scheduled staff meeting was held. When the new senior manager was asked what happened to his predecessor, he said candidly there was a difference of opinion about how the business should be run.

Once the commitment exists to communicate effectively with the staff and that process is in place, management can get on to the issue of communicating with the customer.

## BACK TO BASICS

A knowledgeable staff can definitely enhance customer perceptions of the bank at point of contact, but there are things beyond the control of the contact staff that also influence customer perception. The following story puts the issue in focus.

A bank was conducting consumer research on a new product and brought a group of consumers together to get their reaction. It was carefully explained, with mock-up advertising, letters, and brochures. Most of the group perceived the new product to be more sophisticated than the ones the bank normally offered. One person said, "You know, there aren't even deposit slips or pens in the branch. Now you are asking me to buy a sophisticated new product. Frankly, I'm skeptical."

The bank had lost track of the fact that there are certain basic components of a bank that customers expect to see before they perceive new or exotic service to be deliverable. What are the basics? They represent those things—from the customer's point of view—that indicate the bank is set up to do business. Let's talk about specifics.

*Housekeeping.* Are the public areas of the bank clean and well maintained? Twenty-four-hour ATM areas can be a particular problem. I remember seeing one branch manager early in the morning, picking up litter from the ATM area in her branch. A customer came over to her and said, "You shouldn't be doing that. That's someone else's job." The branch manager said, "It's my business."

*Supplies.* Are deposit slips, pens, envelopes, a date sign, a clock, and other basic supplies that a customer would need available? One bank decided to save money on supplies; the result was that the customers were always complaining to the branch staff.

*Collateral material.* Are the appropriate brochures, application forms, disclosure agreements, and contracts available? One bank was stingy in printing a brochure that described one of its more profitable products. The piece was expensive, but it was all they had to describe the product.

*Signage.* If there are different areas of the branch to do different things, are these areas clearly marked—from the customer's point of view. We have all seen signs that look beautiful but cannot be read or are not understandable because they are written in bankspeak.

*Meeting areas.* Does the branch have a least one confidential meeting area? It could be a conference room or the branch manager's office. Whether it's a conversation between a customer or a staff member, there will be times when privacy is important. One branch did not have a conference room or an office, so all confidential conversations were conducted in the safe-deposit vault. One customer remarked that "The bank can't think much of its staff or customers."

*Communication skills.* Everyone who answers the phone does not have to sound like a BBC announcer. Diction and style are not the issue, but communication is. Someone must decide this is important, select people who can communicate and train them. A related issue is nonverbal communication. The tone of voice or the animation of the body should convey an interest in serving the customer.

*Systems uptime.* Whether it is the ATMs or a system the tellers or platform use, the issue is the same—the customer should perceive that it works. A letter came to the president of a bank complaining that the ATMs were not working. The president responded that the uptime was 99 percent, but the customer wrote back saying that didn't seem to be mathematically possible based on her observations. A second letter from the president made it clear that the uptime pertained to

---

### GUIDE 18
### Identifying the Basics

- What financial services do you currently use (regardless of who supplies them)?

- How do you access your products (telephone, in person, ATM)?

- What problems have you encountered with the products over the last six months?

- What additional product or product features would you like to see?

- What would cause you to buy these new or improved products?

---

all branches, not just the one she was inquiring about. He recognized that systems uptime should be defined from the customer's viewpoint.

Basics can vary across banks, time, and groups of customers. What is basic to one group of customers may be nonessential to others, so it is important to understand the various customer groups. As a start we can ask low, medium, and high profit customers what is basic to them. Guide 18 lists some of the questions we might ask.

From our research we can identify the common conditions, by customer group, that we must satisfy to sell more products. This becomes information that the contact staff can use. Whether it's picking up litter in the ATM lobby or learning more about financial products, the star contact person will act on the information because it affects his or her results.

# Chapter 17

# ASK THE CUSTOMER

A bank invited some of its more profitable customers to a dinner as a way of thanking them and getting some feedback on a new program. The customers mentioned many of the positives associated with the new program and, as the dinner drew to a close, one customer mentioned an issue that the bank was anxious to get feedback on. She said, "I do business with your bank because you not only listen to your customers, you act on their input. It's as if it's our bank."

Maintaining a two-way dialogue with customers is important because it demonstrates that customers are important partners in the creation of service when they interact with the bank. Service is intangible, so we need as much feedback as possible to understand what's good about it and where there is room for improvement. Feedback helps us understand how customers make trade-offs and what factors drive their mind-set; in other words, how the customer makes decisions. An ongoing dialogue can also be useful in developing new product ideas and solutions to problems with current products or services. All in all, dialogue is the best way to detect changes in the market and in our customers.

There are many ways to maintain a dialogue with the customer, but the process starts by collecting information where it is normally generated—at the point where the customer interacts with the bank.

Let's consider the star salespeople in any organization. They routinely, almost unconsciously, collect information about their clients. If we were to ask them why, they would say it helps them to help their clients. We want to get everyone in the bank turned on to this opportunity. The contact manager can be a good point of leverage here as a trainer, as a good listener and questioner (for staff and customers), and as someone who does something with the information.

We can support the information gathering process by ensuring that it is everyone's responsibility to gather information about the customers, and by encouraging direct and immediate response. Immediate feedback can usually clarify issues for both the customer and the contact person. Body language and tone of voice can convey the message that one party doesn't understand or agree with what was said. The other person can then continue to seek closure in a manner that wouldn't be possible in a letter. Immediate feedback has another value: It lets the customer feel that the bank person he or she is dealing with can in fact function as a partner in the creation of service.

In addition to chartering an employee to collect feedback, we can suggest a way to do that and provide support. We can suggest that the contact person maintain a customer feedback report for each customer. This report should contain the customer's name, products owned, products used, and feedback history. On a chronological basis it should indicate the date, nature of the feedback, and action taken on all feedback from the customer. The report form should request specific feedback on products, price, service, and delivery vehicle, as well as general information on what the bank could do to better satisfy the customer's financial needs (see Guide 19). This information should be gathered by the contact person on a regular basis (e.g., every 6 to 18 months) through branch visits, telephone calls, letters, or surveys.

We may not receive incisive feedback every time we contact the customer, but it says we care and maintains a channel of communication. The history is also useful when a customer calls or writes to complain; it becomes a correspondence file that gives us a better insight into the customer so that we can respond in

---

**GUIDE 19**
**Customer Feedback History**

- Customer's name
- Products owned
- Product usage (balance levels, credit, out-standing fees, etc.)
- Feedback history (every 6 to 18 months)
  —dates
  —nature
  —action taken
- Product offering information
  —products
  —price
  —delivery
  —service
- Information about additional needs that could be satisfied
- Action taken

---

a way that focuses on the customer's needs rather than bureau-cratic procedures.

Advisory councils can be another useful source of feedback. The bank's board of directors can function in this role, but if the bank operates in several markets, it might be better to form a group of articulate consumers who represent a cross-section of the market and are interested in receiving better financial services in their market. Management can share information about the bank's mission, vision, plans, results, and concerns. Sharing that type of information is a good way to elicit feedback from the council. The council is also a forum for understanding the marketplace and discerning opportunities. Due to their knowledge of the market and the bank, council members are in a unique position to serve a communication role between the bank and the consumers. This can be a powerful indirect way to communicate with customers.

As mundane as it may sound, merely walking around is a good way to "ask the customer." Successful branch managers do it all the time. Senior managers can do the same thing. An open house once a year in the branch can be a low-cost way to facilitate that type of exchange and at the same time thank customers for their business.

Finally, there will be instances where we need precise, representative, and replicable information from the consumer. The classic case would be new product development. In this instance it pays to get expert counsel to determine how best to do that. While we may know the questions we want input on, how the questions are asked and by whom can be crucial in getting useful results. One bank was researching a new product offering, only to find out in the course of the research that the interviewers were turning off the consumers and the responses had a randomness that suggested indifference. It *was* indifference, but it started on the bank's part. Once they fixed the problem by getting knowledgeable, believable interviewers, they started getting more considered answers.

There is one major danger associated with "Ask the customer," and it's independent of the method of collecting the information. The danger is ignoring the information. If we start asking people's opinions, they will expect to be listened to and reacted to in a manner that makes sense for the business. If we can't do that, we shouldn't start a dialogue that will create expectations we cannot fulfill.

# Chapter 18

# How Profitable
# Are Your Customers?

About ten years ago a consumer bank analyzed its customer base and found that:

- 59 percent of the customers generated a loss.

- 39 percent of the customers generated 37 percent of the profit.

- 2 percent of the customers generated 63 percent of the profit.

The bank recently reexamined its customer base and found that while it had made some progress, about 40 percent of its customers were still unprofitable.

This bank was profitable at both points in time, but the magnitude of the subsidy issue surprised management both times because the bank did not track individual customer profitability. Since the bank was managed on the basis of the total profitability of all its customers, it missed some significant opportunities to manage expenses and revenues in a way that would increase profit. Spending *more* money may have increased the revenue and overall profitability of the high profit customers, whereas for customers the bank lost money on a mixture of decreased expenses and increased revenue may have reduced the drain on profitability.

This profitability problem will only intensify in the coming years: Competition will increase under deregulation, customers will become smarter and more demanding in a price/value sense, real estate expenses will increase, and people costs will grow. In short, the problem won't go away.

After we have estimated the individual profitability of each customer, we can array the data. We will want to do this in two ways: based on our bank's share of each consumer's profitability, and based on the entire profitability generated by each customer. Then we can create four groupings for each array: the unprofitable customers and the remaining customers in three groups, each group accounting for one-third of the total customers (see Guide 20).

| GUIDE 20 | | | | |
| Customer Profitability Distribution | | | | |
| Profit Range | No. of Customers | P+L | % of Customers | % of P+L |
|---|---|---|---|---|
| | | | Unprofitable | |
| | | | Bottom third of the profitable customers | |
| | | | Middle third of the profitable customers | |
| | | | Top third of the profitable customers | |

Now that we know what we have in terms of profitability, we can analyze the data by asking a series of questions from a product-related, expense-related, or de novo perspective.

## PRODUCT-RELATED ISSUES

By analyzing product-related issues we can identify options we could pursue, products we could offer, or customers we could target to serve. Following are key questions to ask:

- What ownership or user changes could we reasonably expect to make and what would the changes in profitability be?

- What would happen if we got all their business for each product?

- Do we currently offer these products? Can we legally offer them?

- What are the potential synergies, e.g., offering a group of products and pricing them as a combined product?

## EXPENSE-RELATED ISSUES

Answers to expense-related questions should give us a better feel for the expense side of the profit equation. They might suggest win/ win solutions or force us to consider modifying the product or not offering it.

- Are there any expense changes we could initiate to make us more efficient (e.g., automation)?

- Are there any trade-offs we might make that would benefit both customers and bank (e.g., offering a better price if a cheaper delivery system is used)?

- Is there a subset of needs for certain customers that could be better met with a less costly delivery system (e.g., the telephone)?

- Is there an opportunity to use or continue a self-service offering?

- Are there some products that won't cover our costs even if reasonable changes were introduced (e.g., safe-deposit boxes)?

- Are there features of products without an explicit cost that might drive excessive use (e.g., free information)?

## DE NOVO ISSUES

Consider what we would do if we entered the market for the first time:

- What business opportunities play to our strengths and our image?

- Where is the win?

- Whom should we target to serve?

- What should our offering be?

- How should we be organized?

- What support systems are needed?

- What is the needed culture?

The product, expense and de novo approaches are all related, but analyzing them separately makes it easier to identify profit opportunities. What should emerge is a clearer sense of how we can better manage our existing customers. The checklist

---

**GUIDE 21**
**Checklist for More Profitably**
**Managing Current Customers**

- How many profitable and how many unprofitable customers do we have?

- What can we do to increase the profitability of both groups?

- Are there certain customers that we can't profitably serve?

- Do we have a system in place to track the profitability of our customers over time?

- Is there a system in place to encourage customers to bring more of their business to us?

---

in Guide 21 offers some questions to consider when analyzing customer profitability.

Actively managing the current mix of customers is a way to increase profitability.

# Chapter 19

# ESTIMATING INDIVIDUAL CONSUMER POTENTIAL

A bank was mounting a sales campaign in which everything was put together competently and creatively. Unfortunately, the bank didn't understand profit potential. In fact, there was no way it could make a profit on half the consumers in its market. As incredible as it may seem, a bank was investing money with no sense of what the return might be. It never tried to estimate the potential profit that consumers in its market could bring to one or more financial service companies. Investment decisions cannot be made without this information, so let's outline a process for getting it. The result will be an estimate, but if it helps us understand that we can't profitably serve 50 percent of our market, it has some value.

Our objective here is to be able to estimate that a given consumer generates X dollars in revenue, Y dollars in associated costs, and Z dollars in profit. These revenues, costs, and profits may be split among several banks or financial service suppliers; we will want to know their respective shares of each consumer's business. In gathering this information we will define a consumer as a household, so we will be analyzing all the financial services a household owns and how they are used. A household may, for example, *own* a credit product, but not *use* it.

We will need information about all the financial services used by households in our market, not just the ones used at our bank. This may involve asking a sampling of consumers in our market questions about balance levels for deposit products, credit in use for loans, average outstanding on credit cards, fees for tax preparation services, and numbers of trades for brokerage products. Exact numbers typically are not obtained because consumers may not know that the average collected balance in their checking account is $594.50, but rather a range, the balance is between $500 and $1,000.

Let's look at Guide 22 and walk through a profitability calculation for one household.

*Step 1* is to calculate the net revenue for each product used. For fee-based products like a safe-deposit box, it's simply the fees charged; for deposit products it is the interest the bank earns on the balance available, plus any other fees (e.g., returned checks), less the interest paid to the consumer, less any other costs, FDIC/FSLIC insurance, reserves that the bank must maintain, and losses. For credit-based products, it would be the interest the consumer pays, plus any other fees

---

**GUIDE 22**
**Calculating Individual Consumer Profit Potential**

*Step 1*  Calculate net revenue generated (by product).
Net revenue generated = interest earned + fees – interest expense – any other costs (e.g., insurance, reserves, losses)

*Step 2*  Calculate expense associated with each product.
Product expense = fixed expense + variable expense

*Step 3*  Calculate household profit potential.
Profit potential = net revenue generated from all products – product expense for all products

---

(e.g., late charges) less the cost of the money to the bank, less any other expenses to the bank (losses). Some of these numbers will come directly from the consumer (balances outstanding, fees paid), some from industry or governmental estimates, and some from estimates based on financial information from our bank.

*Step 2* is to determine the costs of serving the products that the consumer owns. There usually is a fixed cost for owning a product—for instance, the cost of maintaining a safe-deposit box or the cost of maintaining a checking account or a credit account. There is usually also a variable cost based on usage (number of checks written, visits to the branch, use of ATMs, etc.). Based on these costs and the ownership and usage level, we can calculate the cost to serve the consumers.

*Step 3* is to calculate the total profit generated by the household. We do this by subtracting the total costs for each product from the revenue that each product generates and then adding up the difference for each account to calculate individual consumer profitability. While in theory this is fairly easy to do, in practice it can become difficult. It hinges on three questions.

- How frequently should this be done? Initially we might try it on a quarterly basis to gain experience and then decide what frequency is best.

- How do we calculate variable expenses such as branch visits, telephone calls, and mail expenses? We can ask the consumers we sampled questions about their transaction patterns and use industry or our own costs to estimate the variable expense.

- What expenses do we build into our fixed product costs, e.g., the chairman's salary, corporate legal expenses, development expenses, etc. Where the expenses can be directly related to a specific product, perhaps they should be included. By doing it this way it can help us scrutinize all costs that might relate to direct product expense.

Based on the design of the original sample of our marketplace, we can now project the results to our entire market. If the sample is representative of our entire market, then we may be able to multiply the average household profitability from the sample by the total number of households in the market. If the sample was designed to be representative of different types of households (e.g., grouped by income), we may be able to use census or other information in making our projection.

As we repeat this process we may be able to improve its accuracy, but even a crude estimate is better than none. Managing a business without knowing the potential profit is like buying a lottery ticket and not knowing the prize.

# Chapter 20

# LEVERAGING CURRENT CUSTOMERS

As a test, let's estimate what it would cost our bank to cross-sell existing customers additional products versus what it would cost to sell to new customers who have no relationship with the bank. It could be as much as five times as cost-effective to cross-sell existing customers than to find new ones.

Cross-selling is not only cost-effective, it is crucial to executing our mission. Customer profitability is by definition a function of product ownership and usage. By increasing ownership cross-selling enhances profitability. Increased product ownership also promotes loyalty to a bank.

Cross-selling is the most underutilized concept in banking, usually because three conditions are not met: First, the bank must have a way of measuring cross-selling, specifically, how many accounts does each customer have? If we can calculate the customer's profitability, we can calculate accounts/customers. Second, the bank must have meaningful goals in place. This means looking at where we are, where we have been, industry norms, what accounts our target customers have with all suppliers, and then setting a goal. Third, the bank's culture must say cross-selling is at least as important as new accounts. Both are vital to overall profitability.

Once these three conditions are in place, we can make sure that the cross-sell philosophy is reflected in the executional components of the business. These components include:

*Product offering.*    Product offerings should be structured to encourage customers to do more business with the bank. This may be as simple as giving customers a better price when they do more business with us. It also may be designing product offerings so they work synergistically.

*Customer and staff communications.*    If our strategy is to address more than a single need of the consumers, our communications strategy should do the same thing. It should encourage cross-selling by communicating the range and scope of the bank's product offerings.

*Reward systems.*    Since cross-selling is probably the most profit-effective way to grow a business, its importance should be reflected in the reward system for the staff. Reward systems where possible should be profit driven to tie in with the bank's mission of profitably satisfying customers' needs.

A first cousin to cross-selling is selling *all* the bank's services —not just the ones in your department. A bank may be so compartmentalized that each activity is essentially independent of the others. This may mean that customers are rediscovered over and over again, or lost completely.

One branch manager had a rather simple formula for success: He tried to help every customer who came into his branch, regardless of what product the person needed. This often meant referring customers to other bank departments. In time customers thought of him when they had a banking need. He had created shelf space in their mind.

If we are to encourage a smooth hand-off process in our bank, several things have to take place:

- This process should be part of the bank's incentive system.

- Communication between departments should be encouraged so the contact person's network is enlarged.

- The contact staff must be familiar with all the products the bank sells and know where to get—via their network—more information.

- The success rate with closing on this type of business should be tracked.

The natural extension of cross-selling is a referral program. This represents a major opportunity for most businesses. Customers usually know people like themselves, so if we have the right customers for our business, referrals can be an efficient way of identifying new customers. The essential element of a referral program is a consistent level of service.

Banks can encourage referrals in varying ways. Some of the more common vehicles for a referral program are:

- Using an advisory council

- Communicating information of value to the customer

- Sponsoring "bring a friend" seminars

- Supporting cultural events relevant to the target market

- Offering "frequent flyer" type programs for the referees

Confidentiality is sometimes a stumbling block. The sales star is sensitive to this issue and is flexible in how he or she thanks clients.

Leveraging our current customers is something we would do in our own business, so we shouldn't let bureaucracy or culture get in the way at our bank.

# Chapter 21

# Turning Customers into Clients

What is a client? How do you know when you have one? Are they really different from customers? Ask a few and they will say it has less to do with what happens and more to do with a feeling they have about the supplier. If they are guests in a hotel, they will feel at home; if they are in a restaurant, the chef will prepare what they want, naturally.

A client suggests an ongoing business relationship where expectations are normally known and met. The staff know what the client wants. If they don't, they find out and don't forget (see Guide 23).

This relationship has many implications for our business. First, it suggests a preoccupation with the customer; If the mortgage rate is not favorable today and the contact person knows that rate is important, he or she will suggest other options. It also presupposes that the knowledge about a customer's wishes is not lost. The bank keeps a record of the client's feedback. Finally, it suggests an advocacy role. When contact people learn something that may be of interest or value to their clients, they immediately apprise them of it—perhaps merely a phone call about a new product.

The client relationship has both a cost and a value. The service organization must have the client notion in its culture, and must have in place whatever is necessary to execute the concept. This may be a system to record preferences and a commitment to ensure

**GUIDE 23**
**What Is a Client?**

- A client is a customer who has certain expectations and knows that they generally will be met.

- A client is someone who thinks of our bank as his or her bank.

- A client feels at home in our bank.

- A client refers his or her friends to our bank.

- A client understands that mistakes happen, but not often and usually not again.

- A client knows what we stand for.

- A client is a long-term customer.

- A client expects a fair deal.

that the information is independent of any one contact person. Whether people retire or get promoted, the service continues.

The value is that the client over time begins to associate the supplier with a particular product or service. The client might even look to the supplier for advice in that industry—advice that will not be influenced by what the supplier wants, but by the client's needs.

As transfixing as this loyalty may seem, the question is, do we want it? If so, how do we win it and keep it? These questions track back to our vision. If in formulating our vision we talk about being a premier supplier of financial services in our market, the client notion may be interesting but not essential. If the vision suggests we will be the largest or most profitable supplier in our market, the client notion may be even less essential. If, on the other hand, the vision talks about advocacy or suggests that we will be perceived to be the supplier of choice, the notion of clientcy is essential.

Let's assume that our vision encompasses the notion of advocacy—what do we do about it?

First, if we are to treat customers as clients, we must take advantage of all the information the bank has about the client. We cannot have the clients' interests at heart and be their advocate if we don't know what products they have with our bank. Very often the information is useful in suggesting other products clients might need.

Second, it is essential that the contact person keep a record of other useful information. It may be as seemingly trivial as the preferred salutation in a letter to investment preferences. Successful salespeople do this automatically; they never throw out valuable information.

Third, we become more attentive to the time dimension in acquiring a client. It takes longer to develop a client, and the time impacts our profitability. This may be due to repeated sales calls and mailings, or it may suggest a hierarchical relationship between financial service needs. The client may use this hierarchy to test the bank. If the bank is efficient at handling a customer's transactions, the person may after a while decide to see how the bank is at relationship services—i.e., do they manage a group of products owned by the customer in a coordinated fashion? If the answer is positive, the customer may start listening for advocacy signals: Is the contact person offering advice? Is the advice from the customer's point of view? Are some of the small signals, like a holiday card, being sent?

Net, the time required to both mine and measure the development of a client relationship may be far longer and more costly than that needed in a customer relationship. It becomes critical to estimate the final reward. The star salespeople have an innate sense here, and we should ask them to share their experiences. They may not be able to clearly articulate how they allocate their time, but they are stars because they know how to get sales. Knowing how much time to invest in a potential sale is key.

Fourth, in developing and maintaining clients, small things

112

may make the difference. An airline aired a commercial once where they talked about first class. The commercial talked about the small things that differentiate first-class service—sharing information with a client, pointing out pitfalls in the course of action a client is contemplating, or simply addressing someone by his or her name. The sales star understands the power of a name. People like to hear their name. It's a sign of recognition, and it personalizes the communication. The salesperson is talking about an individual, not people in general.

The bank can provide information and resources, but usually it's the contact person who makes first-class real. So we should ask the sales stars how they do it, and get everyone thinking about it.

Fifth, we must be mentally prepared to tell a client "I'm not the best person to do that for you." This in the last analysis may be the key to developing clients and the hardest thing to do. In the increasingly complex and rapidly changing world of financial services, no contact person knows all the answers. But the sales star knows someone who does, and wholeheartedly recommends that person. Our clients are not only customers, they are the focus of our business.

One client maintained a multimillion-dollar relationship with a branch, in fact, really with one contact person. When that person retired, the relationship soon dwindled to a checking account with $150 in it. Soon after the contact person came out of retirement the relationship returned to its former level and the client again started referring his friends. What drove that relationship was not the encyclopedic knowledge of the contact person, but the fact that the client knew he could get consistently reliable advice and execution from the contact person. The contact person had shelf space in the client's mind. It took many years to develop that bond.

Turning customers into clients is truly financial alchemy.

# Chapter 22

# LEARNING FROM THE CUSTOMERS WE LOSE

*American Banker's* 1987 consumer survey suggests there are a number of reasons why consumers change the principal financial institution that they deal with. These include:

- Change in residence
- Service/error
- Locational convenience
- Better interest rates
- Fees too high
- Product range
- Bad advice
- Difficulty getting a loan

The real message is that over half the reasons customers identified were preventable. But let's first see how we can gather this information.

- All customer contact people can on a monthly basis determine why they lost accounts, and in doing so perhaps save some of them.

- Ask new customers why they left their old bank. Given the charter that each customer contact person has, it may be possible to immediately assure new customers that won't happen here, and why.

- On a regular basis, ask our existing customers how they are doing. This is an informal way of getting some open-ended feedback.

- When doing market research, ask customers if they have closed accounts recently and why. This may start giving us an industry wide picture. Maybe we are doing better than our competition in retaining certain groups of customers.

- Monitor letters and calls to the president. They may explain why a customer closed an account or a relationship.

However we get the information, Guide 24 is one way to display it.

What are some of the ways we can stop customers from leaving?

- Comparing the average profitability of new vs. existing customers reinforces the profitability of maintaining and growing customers.

- Monitoring the information captured in the lost customer report and comparing one staff member to another, we may find service stars. Ask them to share their knowledge.

- Providing customers with alternate means of communicating with the bank. (This in turn means encouraging the contact staff to really communicate with management.) One way is to ensure that both customer and staff know who (by name and responsibility) they can talk to and their telephone number and address. This can be an important signal that management is there to support the staff and the business, not merely administer it.

## GUIDE 24
## Lost Customer Report

| Customer Profit Range | Total | Accounts Regrettably Lost | | Relationships Regrettably Lost | | Lost as a % of Total | | Industry Average % of Lost Accounts | |
| --- | --- | --- | --- | --- | --- | --- | --- | --- | --- |
| | | Number of Account | Average Age | Number of Account | Average Age | Accounts | Relationships | Accounts | Relationships |

- Encouraging cross-sell. Customers generally are less likely to leave a bank if they have multiple accounts with the bank. Loyalty can encourage customers and staff to resolve problems rather than walk away from them.

- Establishing an advisory board to get some of the more influential customers involved in the business. They may be a good source of feedback and can alert management to potential problems.

- Changing our product offering to reduce the runoff of customers.

Actively managing the issue of customer runoff is fundamentally dependent upon management saying that customers are important. If they are, management won't want to lose them. The danger is that a bank will focus on new customers and not grow the ones it has. In order to be successful, we must do both.

# Chapter 23

# IMPACTING CUSTOMER BEHAVIOR

Since customers provide the revenue for our business, one central question is, How can we impact customers' behavior so that they will bring us more profit? Guide 25 can help us think about how to impact customer behavior. It illustrates that there are four factors operating in the decision-making process: facts, perceptions, trade-offs, and mind-set.

The table at the bottom of the guide suggests that it is hardest to change a customer's mind-set and easiest to provide facts. This can help us allocate resources most effectively. Let's consider facts first.

## FACTS

This can be the easiest of the four factors to address, providing customers with information that will help them make their financial decisions, but there are some issues to face nonetheless.

The sheer magnitude of the information that a customer could request is awesome. A bank may offer hundreds of products or services, each one with options, conditions, and rates. These may change daily, weekly, or with no particular schedule. If the medium does not exist to access these produces, the investment the bank has made in them cannot be fully recovered. At some point in a customer transaction, the contact person must be able either to effi-

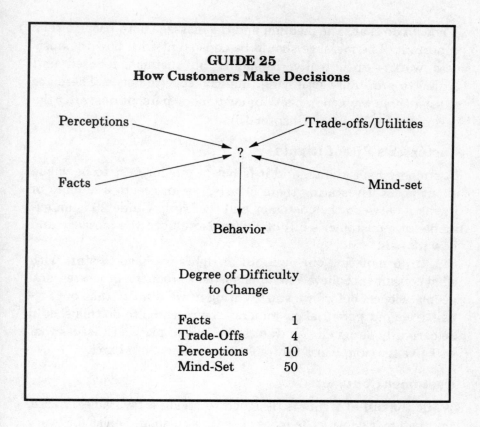

**GUIDE 25**
**How Customers Make Decisions**

Perceptions

Trade-offs/Utilities

?

Facts

Mind-set

Behavior

Degree of Difficulty
to Change

| | |
|---|---|
| Facts | 1 |
| Trade-Offs | 4 |
| Perceptions | 10 |
| Mind-Set | 50 |

ciently access the information or smoothly hand off the customer. If the bank doesn't do this, the customer will. We don't want to set up an environment in which the customer becomes captive of the bank's culture in the event that the staff person with the information is ill. Information must be set free and used as an investment in the business. The solution to this problem starts with equipping the contact person with useful and readily accessible data.

## PERCEPTIONS

"We are what we pretend to be, so we must be careful what we pretend to be." (Kurt Vonnegut, Jr., *Mother Night*) The question is how to do that. The medium and the message both become very important. The message should be consistent with how the business works—specifically, it should be customer-focused and geared to profitably satisfying financial service needs. There are at least three ways to impact our customers' perceptions, *after* the basics are in place (see Chapter 16).

## Customer's Bill of Rights

Customers have rights, and it is not in our interest to be vague about them. By stating them clearly, we an create a climate of fairness between the customer and the bank. Guide 26 is an example of a customer's bill of rights. Note both the message and how it's said.

In formulating our own bill of rights we have to start with what consumers believe about banks, their products, processes, and people. Hence, before we start writing it, we want to take our signals from our potential customers. The research to do this should be carefully designed. We want to be able to play back issues that will give the customer a favorable impression of our bank.

## Customer Contract

While the bill of rights is designed to create a favorable climate, the customer contract is more specific and should exist for every product the bank sells. The contract should specify what the bank agrees to do and what the customer agrees to do (see Guide 27). However potentially valuable the contract may be in creating a favorable perception, it must be understood by the average customer. So, after it is written, test it on some real customers.

The positive message we are looking to send with the contract is that there will be no surprises. The customer doesn't have to ask the right question in the right way to the right person. The bank has the technical expertise here. Leverage it, don't hide it. The contract should also outline any post-contract rights, such as renewal privileges. When the contract is signed, both parties should understand what the process is to resolve disagreements: first, an

## GUIDE 26
## Customer's Bill of Rights

*Definition:*   A simply and clearly stated list of expectations that a customer can look forward to.

*Guidelines:*

- Addresses basic concerns that a customer might have about transactions and relationships.
- Conveys tangible and intangible aspects.
- Is clearly and simply written.
- Is broad enough to accommodate change over time.

*Example:*

- I will be treated with respect.
- I will be communicated with directly, simply, accurately, and in timely fashion.
- I will know all the terms and conditions when I am deciding to purchase and will have a record for my information.
- The best deal will automatically be brought to my attention.
- The bank will attempt to address my needs, concerns, and questions, even if I don't ask the right question.
- There will be a clear statement of the standards for normal interaction.
- I will receive a service guarantee.
- I will clearly understand the appeal process.
- It will be in my interests to bring more profitable business to the bank.

---

**GUIDE 27**
**Customer Contract**

*Definition:* An open and fair agreement specifying the rights and responsibilities of all parties.

*Guidelines:*

- Is simply written and easy to understand.
- Spells out responsibilities (including penalties) of both parties.
- Contains no surprises.
- Outlines post-contract rights.
- Specifies appeal process.

*Example:*

The bank agrees to:

The customer agrees to:

Nonagreements will be arbitrated by the XYZ Arbitration Service Inc.

_____          _____
Customer                         Bank

---

internal appeal process within the bank, then the involvement of a third party.

## Service Guarantee

Included in the purchase price of a product is usually some amount and level of service. What we want to do here is *specify* what that is

## GUIDE 28
### Service Guarantee

*Definition:*   Specific, where possible measurable, list of standards that the bank will meet and the penalty it will pay if it does not.

*Guidelines:*

- Is transaction-specific.
- Conveys an expectation level.
- Includes all products or services offered.
- Explains relevant penalties.

*Example* (for a checking account):

- Deposits will be posted the next business day.
- Customer will receive a clear statement of when funds are available.
- Statements will be mailed, _____ day(s) after statement closing date.
- Financial inquiries/complaints will be assured in _____ days.
- Nonfinancial inquiries (balances, check clearance) will be answered immediately.
- Other nonfinancial inquiries will be answered in _____ days.
- If standards are not met, the customer has choice of $_____ or $_____ fees waived.

by first defining it, then stating a standard that we will meet, and finally indicating what the penalty is if we don't meet the standard. We want to guarantee the elements of service that the customer is most interested in, not what the bank thinks the customer is interested in, or worse, what the bank wishes to use as a standard. Each product should have a specific service guarantee. The standards that make up the guarantee and the actual results should be reported every month for each client. This information belongs in the bank's annual report.

A word about penalties: Whatever the penalties are, the customer should be able to receive them immediately and simply, when this is possible. In terms of arriving at what the penalties are, we should ask the consumers for their thoughts here; they are designed for them. Guide 28 is an example of a service guarantee.

One overall comment about perceptions: The key here is to get the customers to play back their perceptions so we can understand and influence them. While research here is important, feedback from the contact staff may be more relevant because they pick up information when the perceptions are being formed, and may be able to influence them.

## TRADE-OFFS

If we were putting together a sales plan for an existing product, one of the first questions we might ask is what feature of the product is most important to our target customers. Depending on the product, the potential list could be extensive, e.g., price, 24-hour access, our guarantee, ease of opening the account, or information available. Even if we knew which feature was generally the most important to our target customers, how does that one feature relate to the others? Is price twice as important as the next preferred feature, 24-hour access, and are the other features relatively unimportant —as long as they are there and work. Trade-off information can be a crucial part of influencing customer behavior.

Guide 29 is an example of the type of information we would

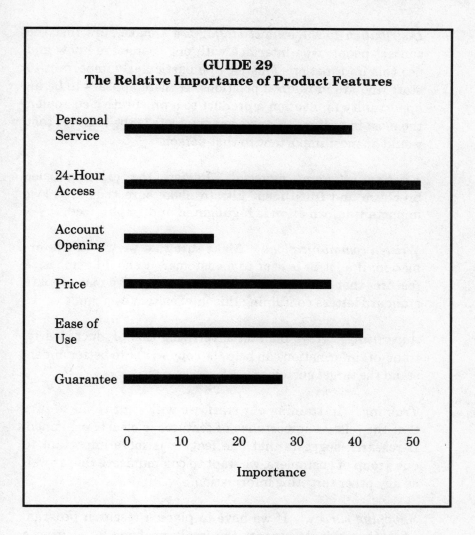

**GUIDE 29**
**The Relative Importance of Product Features**

like to have. This will require some market research,[1] but first research the contact staff.

Let's assume that we have completed the research—what do we do with it?

[1]Paul Green and Jerry Wind, "New Ways to Measure Consumer's Judgment," *Harvard Business Review,* July–August 1975.

*Distribution to the contact staff.* Let's make sure that the contact people who interface with our customers know and use this information. This may be particularly important to staff who are in referral positions. If there appears to be an opportunity to mention a product to a prospective customer, the most important thing to communicate is the features that would be most important to that person.

*Existing collateral material.* Review the existing sales brochure and fulfillment kits to make sure that the most important information is highlighted and emphasized.

*Written communications.* Make sure that we use this information; if a letter is sent to a customer, it should emphasize features that are important to the customer. We may prepare standard letters containing this information as a guide.

*Advertising.* If we plan on advertising this product clearly, trade-off information can help the copy writer to better understand the target customer.

*Training.* In training our staff, we will want to make sure that the relative importance of features is clearly explained. If research suggests that one feature is more important to one group of customers, we want to communicate this as well as any other targeting information.

*Shopping survey.* If we have in place a research program where individuals contact the bank, perhaps by visiting a branch and inquiring about various products, we want as part of their report feedback on what features of the products are stressed. It is not enough that a product is mentioned by the staff; it should be sold in the manner most designed to affect a sale.

## MIND-SET

This is normally the most intractable area of customer behavior to impact because we may not know what their mind-set is. We know they will probably want some facts to make decisions, but we may not know what the basic forces guiding their decisions are. Examples of these are:

Customers may prefer to deal with several banks because they feel it's safer or more confidential, or because they want to have an alternate source in case of an emergency.

Some customers may prefer to talk to a person in a service environment, while others may not. One customer in a focus group was very positive about ATMs because there were no value judgments, role playing, or nonverbal communications. Other customers may not like automated services because of vision problems, fear of technology, impersonality, or reluctance to change.

There may be a built-in factor that encourages some customers to buy insurance from an insurance company, traditional bank products from a bank, investment advice from a financial adviser, etc. These basic forces, whatever they may be, may be changeable—if we know what they are. Sometimes this information can be gleaned from asking the consumer financial attitude questions of the kind discussed in Chapter 5. We will need some expert guidance here to explore the issues effectively.

The customer contact staff may also be able to guide us in exploring the issues. They may have a sense based on customer interactions what some of the mind set issues are. The sales star is probably very adept at getting at the information. If he or she did not understand mind set, they probably would not close as many sales as they do.

However we get the information that is relative to our market, what do we do about it?

Share the information in sales meetings.   During our regular sales meetings we can encourage the staff to share some of their recent experiences, information, and action ideas that work for them in overcoming mind-set obstacles. For example, the salesperson's skillful questions coupled with a demonstration or relevant testimonial may have been the key to someone using an ATM or a direct deposit service.

Use role playing with mind-set as the focus.   This can help the person playing the customer and the one playing the sales-person to understand the issues and overcome them.

Use advisory groups to get information.   Asking people what their mind-set is may not be productive, but discussing a product with a group of consumers or our advisory board may be. For example, management could say, "We are having problems selling product X, which should be a good need satisfier to our target audience." After reviewing product X and discussing the features, we could ask the advisory board to put themselves in the target customers' role and see if they can think of any potential sales objection. If they don't comment on mind-set issues, we can at least mention some of the common ones and get their reaction.

If we sense that there is a certain group of customers who share a mind set we would like to change, we may be able to work with an affinity group. By focusing on the potential benefit to their group, we may elicit both input and support, perhaps an article in their magazine about the service and how pleased the customers were.

Free trial may also work here. By encouraging the customer to try it, we may even be able to get a testimonial.

In summary, we can use a wide array of techniques to impact customer behavior, but they will all be of limited value if we don't *focus on the customer.*

# MANAGING THE CUSTOMERS AND THE STAFF

# Chapter 24

# DESIGNING AN ORGANIZATION TO FIT THE MISSION

After we have come to peace with our mission statement and fleshed it out with a strategy, we should think about what organizational structure will be most effective in executing the mission and the strategy. Some banks have elected to take the high profit segment we talked about in the last chapter and form a separate organization to serve these customers (e.g., a private banking department).

The question really is, What organizational structure is best for our bank? The answer depends upon the mission, strategy, competition, and culture of our bank. Indeed, what may be an effective organization for a bank at one point in time may not be at another. If the same bank serves different marketplaces, it may be more effective to have a different organizational structure in each market.

If our mission is to serve many different groups of customers, our structure should reflect this. If we are planning on satisfying a relatively small number of consumer needs, perhaps our support groups (marketing, operations, etc.) should be one single entity. If our vision is high tech, we may need a group that focuses on these issues. If it is "high touch," i.e., an emphasis on one-on-one customer interaction, we may need a more extensive human resources function. Net, the question is, What are the major groups of people and skills needed to execute our mission and vision? The organization should reflect the answer to this question.

The maximum number of people should be in customer contact roles, and everyone in the organization should be as close as possible to the interaction with the customer. Organization charts should start not with the CEO, but with the customer, the source of revenue. If the people who directly affect the customer are five layers removed from the customer, we cannot respond to the customer's needs in a timely fashion. Several smaller units that face off against groups of customers may be more effective than one large group.

Along these same lines, the minimum number of interfaces should exist. The more people involved in meeting a customer's need, the harder it is to manage the process. But, more importantly, the process can sometimes overshadow customer needs. Collapsing interfaces or automating certain functions may help here.

The structure should be simple to understand. One bank had its branch staffs organized so that there were three different units in the branch and no single branch manager. The customers were forced to liaison between the different units to get anything accomplished.

A bank needs a critical mass of key managers so that if one person leaves the bank won't collapse. The structure should have its own disaster recovery program built in. Several smaller units can help here.

The structure should be capable of growth. If we are successful in growing the business or acquire another bank, can we continue to use the present organization? Every time there is a reorganization the staff will be focusing on that and not the customers, so we should get one that we can live with for a while.

Probably the most important thing to keep in mind when designing an organization is profitability. If we know that individual profitability of most people in the bank, we can not only more profitably manage the business, but we can better manage the number of people required and, in turn, the required structure. Next time you see an organization structure, try to pencil in the profitability that a group of people produces. It will help you manage the organization more profit-effectively.

I visited a bank many years ago that had about a thousand employees and twelve levels between the first level of customer contact and the CEO. The bank had a reputation for being very well run because it was the market leader with little aggressive competition. The customers that were there wanted to be there, and it had a reputation for caring. Well, the bank management did care, but they cared about control. The bank decided what it wanted to offer in the way of products and put in place an efficient system (from the bank's point of view) with lots of people supervising its execution. When deregulation came along, the bank hit some rough times because its culture was not focused on the customer and its structure made change very difficult.

The real issue in organizational design is not "Do we have the perfect one?" but "Why do we have the one we do?" If we can't answer that question, we probably have a problem that extends far beyond the structure of the organization and touches on what are we here to do. At that point you want to go back to the mission statement and make the organization compatible with it.

# Chapter 25

# FITTING THE EMPLOYEE ROLES TO THE ORGANIZATION

Several years ago, as part of a reorganization, a bank conducted a study on the role of tellers. Tellers and their managers were interviewed, as well as customers who used teller services. What emerged was something of a surprise, for each group had significantly different views on the principal role of the teller.

- The tellers themselves perceived that their principal role was to avoid losses. They rarely mentioned anything that related to satisfying customers' needs or that suggested they were part of a business to *profitably* satisfy customers' needs. They perceived that they were in the transaction business, where great care must be taken to avoid errors.

- Management, in discussing the role of tellers, barely mentioned the operating losses, even though in the poorly managed branches this occupied a considerable amount of their time. Losses were almost accepted as a given in the overall branch process. Perhaps that was one reason they were so high. The teller roles they did stress related to human relations skills that they thought the customers wanted. Smiling, being cordial, and calling people by their name were things the managers thought the tellers should be doing.

- Customers shared the transactional notion with tellers, but it focused more on efficiency. They were interested in the teller completing their transaction as quickly as possible. Errors were not frequently volunteered as a concern. In fact, even when errors were specifically asked about, they usually weren't seen as a problem. Tellers standing at their stations but not open for business was a sign of inefficiency to some customers.

It became obvious that the customers received what the tellers felt was their job. This did not reflect any recognition of what business the bank was in, the vision of the specified bank, and the mission of profitably satisfying customer needs. Again, in retrospect it is obvious that those three issues were never discussed with the tellers because management had never addressed them. Roles should be consistent with the business and clearly defined. In this chapter we will discuss five salient roles: contact staff, contact manager, support staff, support manager, and senior manager.

## CONTACT STAFF

The contact people are the window to the bank. They directly interface with the customers in person, over the telephone or by letter. They may be tellers, platform people, customer sales reps, service center reps, telephone operators, guards, secretaries, floor walkers, or operations people. Whatever they are called, there is a commonality in what they must do to profitably serve customers' needs. One is to create a favorable impression of what the bank can be to the consumer. The second is to satisfy customers' needs.

Jerry Martens was good at doing both things. He had about 20 years' experience with a foreign bank. Several years after he started with his new bank and had achieved remarkable success, someone asked him the secret of his success. Martens wasn't sure, but he attributed it in part to his experience. When he was opening a new branch for a foreign bank, perhaps the only branch in that city, he had to make sure that every contact with a customer was developed to the fullest. Consequently, he not only personally focused on this issue, but encouraged his staff to do so also. In the orientation program he put together for new people he pointed out with pride that the foreign bank had a well-developed support capability. He also talked about (and had a pamphlet that described) the history of the bank, its vision, and its plans. He said they couldn't represent the bank unless they knew that and unless they had a charter to spell out their responsibility and authority.

The contact staff must be able to execute transactions. Depending on the job, it could involve a fair amount of training, resources, customer information, product information, and operational support. The support should be user-friendly, fast, efficient, and reliable. It is sometimes appropriate to refer a customer to another contact person—perhaps someone to open an account, prepare a trust, or discuss tailoring credit to the customer's needs. Jerry Martens' point here was not to lose the customer in the referral process.

Profitably satisfying customer needs is not an automatic process. Someone has to manage the relationship between each customer and the bank. The amount of time and resources needed to do so depend on the customer and the perceived potential. The contact staff usually are in the best position—by virtue of their knowledge about the customer, the bank and the market—to make this call, but they need the support listed in Guide 30.

The contact staff also may pick up or initiate action that results in feedback. We don't want to lose any useful feedback, whether it comes from a safe-deposit clerk or a receptionist.

To make the most of these "moments of truth," Jan Carlzon's wonderful phrase, when customers interact with the contact staff, the staff must be customer focused with good interpersonal, sales, and service skills.

## GUIDE 30
## Contact Staff Roles

*What They Must Do to Make the Business Work*

- Function as window to the bank.
- Execute transactions.
- Make referrals to other sales staff.
- Manage individual customer profitability.
- Secure feedback from customers.

*Skills Needed*

- Customer focused
- Interpersonal skills
- Sales
- Service
- Emotional energy

*Support Needed*

- History, vision, and plans of bank
- Personal charter
- Customer information
- Product information
- Operational support
- Customer profitability report
- Service monitoring report
- Customer feedback report
- Customer communication capability

## CONTACT STAFF MANAGERS

The contact staff manager could be a branch manager, a private banking team leader, or a sales or service manager. Guide 31 highlights the role.

One of the manager's major responsibilities is selecting contact people. Most of the skills needed are not easily measured— a willingness to serve or meet needs, good interpersonal skills, a talent for selling. A person's effectiveness is often influenced by the clientele and contact manager. In the last analysis, the skills will have to be observed in practice to be verified. For these reasons, the contact manager is normally the best person to make and maximize personnel selection decisions.

For similar reasons the contact manager is usually the best person to develop and reward the staff. To be effective, development programs must address the strengths and weaknesses of the individual. What one person would like for a reward may be quite different from another. The effective contact manager treats everyone, customer and staff, individually.

The contact manager is also in the best position to make resource decisions because he or she knows the market, the staff, and the customers. These decisions could involve hours of operation, number and type of personnel, marketing programs, and contribution to not-for-profit organizations. With the resource authority comes profitability responsibility for their unit.

The effectiveness of the contact staff managers can be influenced by the quality of the support they receive; hence it is in their own interests, as well as the bank's, to maintain an ongoing dialogue with the support staff. The contact manager can also provide feedback to the support staff on how well they are doing.

In many cases the contact manager will be a branch manager. In addition to the roles discussed above, the branch manager can function as a "branch president"—someone the consumer perceives as a senior officer who has power and influence within the bank and the community. This often is the key to

## GUIDE 31
### Contact Staff Managers' Role

*What They Must Do to Make the Business Work*

- Select, develop and reward staff.
- Allocate resources.
- Manage (controllable) profitability of unit.
- Maintain profit-effective dialogue with support staff.
- Bank "president" or presence manager.

*Skills Needed*

- Entrepreneurial
- Sales
- Service
- Operations
- Customer focused
- High energy level

*Support Needed*

- Personal charter
- History, vision, plans of bank
- Support staff managers
- Service monitoring report
- Customer feedback report
- Market share report
- Customer profitability report
- Senior manager's support

growing the business of a branch, and involves a sense of owner-ship on the manager's part.

The potential win for the bank is tremendous. "Half the na-tion's 50,000 bank and thrift branches are unprofitable" (*American Banker* 10/14/87, p.30). "But with some common sensical fixes the great majority of these can be turned around." (*American Banker* 2/17/88, p.1). The six areas for opportunity highlighted were:

- Unintended fee waiving
- Unprofitable accounts
- In-branch efficiency
- Intrabank expenses
- Regional administration
- Undifferentiated branch management

Branch managers can affect most of these areas. They need many skills, but most of all they must think like and be rewarded like entrepreneurs. They also need the support of senior managers.

## SUPPORT STAFF

The support staff would include a variety of functions, data proc-essing, marketing, legal, credit, and administrative services. Most support staffers have no direct reports (with the possible excep-tion of a secretary) and do not normally interface with customers (see Guide 32). They are usually involved in three generic activi-ties. One is to provide timely, efficient, and accurate transactional service for the customer. Two is to provide information, expertise, and advice to staff and customers. Three is to provide research, development, delivery, creative, and administrative services.

The technical or professional skills needed by the support staff are quite diverse. These skills are usually relatively easy to identify or a requirement for the position; if we need legal advice, normally

## GUIDE 32
## Support Staff Role

*What They Must Do to Make the Business Work*

- Deliver timely, efficient and accurate transaction service for customer.
- Provide information, expertise and advice to staff and perhaps customers.
- Provide research, development, delivery, creative, and administrative service.

*Skills Needed*

- Specific to assignment (e.g., technical, legal, marketing, etc.)
- Ability to stay customer focused

*Support Needed*

- Personal charter
- History, vision, plans of bank
- Operational support
- Feedback from contact staff
- Support manager

we would look for someone with a law degree. There is another less tangible skill that is required, and that is the need to stay customer focused. One of the great dangers that any service organization faces is becoming "introverted," as Carlzon termed it, "becoming an organization that loses its conceptual focus on customers' needs as critically important to success . . . If only the customers would go away and leave me alone, I could get my job done." seems to be the attitude. (Albrecht & Zemke, p.23)

This danger is most likely to start with the support staff, because they never see a customer. There are several things we can do about that. One is to involve them directly with the customer where possible. Where this is not possible, at least provide feedback from the customer. This may be feedback of a general nature or ideally about the job or area the particular staff member works in. Also on a regular basis, the support staff should receive from senior managers a status report on the business, how we are doing, where we are going. Merely having the support staff meet the contact staff face to face can be beneficial. So when there are staff meetings, have all the employees that service a given group of customers meet together, whether they report to the same vice president or not.

It's the support that provides the opportunity for a bank to truly differentiate itself.

## SUPPORT STAFF MANAGERS

The support staff managers would include marketing managers, operations managers, systems managers, or anyone that manages a group of people that typically do not interface with the customer. (See Guide 33.)

The staff support manager plays an important role here in both managing a support unit on a day-to-day basis and in selecting, developing and rewarding the staff. So it becomes critical for the support staff manager to interview and be the final word on their new staff. This encourages them to both explore the customer focus issue with new staff and manage it. Some of the attributes we discussed earlier in this chapter on selecting contact can be also useful in selecting support staff.

There are many things that they must do to make the business work, but the most important and often the most difficult is to manage the delivery of *profit*-effective support services. This is easier said than done because often their efforts cannot easily be

## GUIDE 33
## Support Staff Manager Role

*What They Must Do to Make the Business Work*

- Provide profit effectiveness support services.
- Secure feedback from contact and support staff.
- Allocate resources.
- Select, develop, and reward staff.
- Manage expense of unit.

*Skills Needed*

- Profit focus
- Innovative use of resources
- Sensitivity to customer's needs

*Support Needed*

- Personal charter
- History, vision, plans of bank
- Contact staff manager
- Senior managers
- Operational support
- Customer information
- Consumer profitability report
- Customer service monitoring report

related to specific revenue dollars. The temptation then is to simply manage the expenses associated with providing the support services.

Clearly, expenses are important in any business, but in the consumer banking business they are becoming more and more important due to deregulation and increased competition, but also due to the shrinking margin and escalating costs. But we are not in business to minimize expenses but to profitably satisfy the financial needs of our customers. If the support manager is not committed to this, the danger is that the support unit may become introverted. Establishing the link, then, between revenue and expenses becomes crucial.

The support manager also needs feedback from the contact staff and customers about the customers' perception of the support service. With this feedback the support manager can get some sense that a need is being satisfied, and hopefully input on how it could be better satisfied. This facilitates allocating resources, managing expenses, and innovation.

One of the exciting challenges of the support manager may be innovation. This can be making a product more user friendly, designing a delivery system that better meets the needs of the consumer, developing a new product, etc. The support manager needs to be attentive to the opportunities and creative in outlook.

## SENIOR MANAGERS

Who are the senior managers? Those individuals who have the responsibility of orchestrating the resources and results of the bank as a whole over time. The systems nature of the business, the intangible nature of the output and the organizational distance from the point revenue is generated, all make it essential that senior management be truly stars. But what do they have to do to make the business work? Guide 34 highlights the role of senior managers.

Senior managers must give some sense of meaning to what the bank is all about and it shouldn't be a secret. Tangible signs of this include the vision and mission statement of the bank and the charter for each staff member. Having them is one thing, making

# GUIDE 34
## Senior Managers' Role

*What They Must Do to Make the Business Work*

- Establish, communicate, and execute the vision, mission, and charters of the bank.
- Provide resource, personal, and emotional support.
- Grow the culture.
- Select, develop, and reward staff.
- Manage change and innovation.
- Make the investment decisions.

*Skills Needed*

- Communication
- Motivation
- Customer focus
- Commitment
- Consistency
- Leadership
- Service attitude

*Support Needed*

- Personal charter
- History, vision, plans of bank
- Market share report
- Staff
- Customer profitability report
- Service monitoring report
- Customer feedback report

sure that they have been effectively communicated to the staff, customers, and general public is another. In gathering feedback from these three groups, we should have them play back what we're all about—it's perceptions that count.

Senior managers also have the ability by their example and actions to reinforce the bank's focus on the customer. One important way they can do that is to support the customer interaction process. Not administer it, but support the people who make the money for the bank.

The *growing* of a culture is one of the senior manager's most challenging jobs. But it's at the heart of an organization; what the contact people think and believe can significantly impact the results of the business. Culture can be felt, so the good senior manager has his or her antenna out when walking around.

The senior manager like any manager has a responsibility for selecting, developing, and rewarding staff in a manner that is consonant with the missions of the bank. Unfortunately, this isn't a science but attitudes and past performance may be a useful guide.

Managing change and innovation is another one of those things that's easy to talk about, but harder to do; it certainly can't be achieved by fiat. But growing the right culture can help, as can providing the required resources, and personal and emotional support.

The short list of the skills that will be particularly valuable in the bank include communication, motivation, customer focus, commitment, consistency, and leadership. One essential thing they need is the support of the staff; it's the staff that directly or indirectly interfaces with the customer and generates the profits.

We have discussed in this chapter five key roles in the bank, and as Katz and Kahn have said, "the organization is a system of roles." It's important that they be consistent with the business, well defined and clearly communicated.

The danger is that the roles serve the people in the organization, not the customers. Getting the role clearly defined and practiced can help avoid that problem.

# Chapter 26

# SUPPORTING THE CUSTOMER INTERACTION

The fourth principle for success, explained in Chapter 1, is that customer interaction is the key to successful consumer banking. To implement that principle three things are essential: developing an appropriate personal attitude, selecting the right people, and supporting them. This means that the manager must give up "being an administrator who loves to run others and become a manager who carries water for his people on the job."[1]

Managers can impact price and distribution, but the people who generate the money to pay salaries and stockholders' dividends are the people who interface with customers. Since the managers are not there during most of the "moments of truth," the best they can do is support that interaction. Guide 35 attempts to capture the essence of what the manager's job is all about.

What are the characteristics of the right contact people?

- *The ability to think and be rewarded like an entrepreneur.* No one can be a partner in the service partnership if they do not feel it's their business and what they do is important. They have to be proactive, the buyer may say no but their objective is to profitably satisfy the needs of their customers, and sometimes the customer is not sure how to proceed.

[1]Robert Townsend, *Further Up the Organization* (Knopf, 1984), p. xiii.

**GUIDE 35**
**Manager's Creed**

- Being someone people can trust
- Understanding the business
- Showing commitment to the business
- Setting a personal example and following through
- Willing to do the essentials, glamorous or menial
- Searching mind for input and guidance
- Ensuring that no disincentives develop
- Adopting a long-term focus
- Avoiding pomp and circumstances
- Picking the right people
- Backing the people who are doing the right things
- Being a cheerleader
- Making sure that the right people are rewarded or protected for doing the right things
- Paying attention to detail

- *The ability and disposition to make decisions.* The contact staff are the ones that are interfacing with customers; hence, within their authority and responsibility they have to be able and willing to make decisions that will impact both the customers and the bank.

- *The willingness and ability to serve.* Whether it's the teller or the CEO, if they are not emotionally prepared to serve a customer, they are in the wrong business.

- *A predisposition to be involved with people.* The last thing that a service business needs is a brilliant introvert facing off with their customers, except of course if it's another brilliant introvert as a customer. The contact person must be predisposed to interact with people.

- *Good inter-personal skills.* The contact person must be adept at all forms of communication, including non-verbal communication. It's in this area that the service star excels.

- *A good network.* The contact person cannot be expected to know everything that the customer may require, but will have an extensive network of people who can be of assistance.

- *A predisposition to selling themselves.* In many instances the contact persons will first have to establish themselves in the eye of the customers before they can sell the bank's product and meet customers needs.

- *An aptitude to solve problems, perhaps by going around them.* Satisfying customers needs may require bending a rule here or there. The contact person must know where that is required and be prepared emotionally to do it.

- *Emotional and physical stamina.* Interfacing with people is demanding. Often the contact person feels he is on stage, "up" all the time; he needs the energy to do that.

- *Lastly, the wonderful ability to put yourself in your customer's shoes as you are talking to the customer.*

The above list of characteristics may seem overwhelming, but a contact person who is a star has these traits and more.

If we have selected the right people, we must be prepared to support them. What are the essential action steps that management can take to support the right people?

- *Providing a vision and a charter to each staff member in a manner that it is understandable and actionable.*

- *Creating a culture that is consistent with the nature of the business.* Chester Barnard [2] was probably one of the first management writer/CEOs to talk about creating the social values in an organization as one of the major responsibilities of the CEO.

- *Providing the right tools.* There are some basic resources that represent the minimum essentials to be in the business: an operating support system, information about customers, and information about the bank's products and competitors. If we don't have them, it becomes very difficult to profitably satisfy the customers' needs.

- *Ensuring a personnel support system is in place.* This system is designed to meet the needs of the bank staff and represents more than an assortment of employee benefits. It is based on the assumption that how management treats the employees is how the employees will treat the customer. So the personnel support system represents a commitment to the employees.

- Putting in place a real reward system. If we are in the business of profitably serving our customers' needs, we should be able to recognize and reward individual staff members' contributions to individual customer profitability. Where this isn't possible in support or development activities, other measures that relate to profitably satisfying customers' needs shall be developed, e.g., timeliness, quality or efficiency standards, or new need-satisfying products.

  The management star knows that rewards are more than financial; they include recognition, respect, personal

[2]Barnard was president of New Jersey Bell Telephone Company, the United Services Organization (USO), and the Rockefeller Foundation. He wrote *The Functions of an Executive* (Harvard University Press, 1938).

growth, time off when needed, a caring environment, etc. The best reward, though, is what the individual wants as a reward; the management star finds out and tries to deliver.

- *Lastly, management must be personally supportive.* There may be a "well done," picking up a piece of paper in the bank, or defending the service star. It's an individual action that the manager takes that demonstrates a personal commitment.

This chapter discussed some specific ways in which management can support the customer's interaction with the bank. But the real message is that management must feel that is its principal role.

The danger is that managers will feel their job is administering the bank and be at cross purposes with the real nature of the business of profitably meeting the customers' needs as they interact with the bank.

# Chapter 27

# MAKING THE EMPLOYEES ENTREPRENEURS

Robert Townsend said it in *Further Up the Organization,* but deep down, we all know it . . . people work at about 20 percent of their capacity. Why not set a goal of doubling the efficiency, which would still be less than 50 percent, but how can we go about doing that? Three ways: removing the disincentives, providing incentives, and planning capacity.

A disincentive is something that exists within the organization that impedes the execution of the mission. The disincentives that we will concentrate on here are the ones that a bank's own management put in place and hence can remove.

What are some of the classic disincentives?

*Vagueness in defining each employee's job and charter.* If the job really is to reduce expenses, let's say that. In the long run, clarity will be much more economical in time, money, and morale.

*Putting the wrong person in the wrong job.* A sales star may not be a systems star. A superb customer's man may not be nearly as effective as a manager. Get the right person in the right job and then sort out the salary, job rotation, and control issues.

*Designing systems from everyone's point of view except the customer's.* One bank put in a new system for investigations. The branch would call, leave a recorded message, and the investigation department would work on it. The system didn't work too well because there was no way for the contact person to follow up without making another call. The system was finally stopped when it collapsed of its own weight; each investigation generated five to ten follow-up investigations.

*Frequent reorganizations and organizations that create friction.* If several departments think that they are responsible for training, probably very little effective training will take place.

*Poor or no support.* Whether it relates to systems or protecting the risk taker, if management doesn't provide support, the staff will figure out a way. If management doesn't provide the needed MIS for cross-selling, it won't happen. If risk takers are not supported, there won't be any innovation.

*Not managing the culture. For example, maintaining the class/ clan system in the bank*—vice presidents talking only to vice presidents, officials only getting business cards, rewards independent of personal results, better dining facilities for officers, elaborate use of titles.

The list could go on and on, but when you are reviewing expenses, ask the question, Does this help the bank profitably serve its customers? In your daily interactions with other employees, ask yourself the same question. Culture can be changed.

We need an engine to drive our business, one that drives profit generation. A reward system that relates personal results to personal rewards can be such an engine. Establishing this link sends the message that we are committed to profitably serving the customers' needs. It is now more than the mission of the business—it becomes the engine that drives the business.

For the contact staff, we can measure customer profitability and use that as a guide. For support activities where it is difficult to relate individual customer profitability to the person's results, we can develop other measures that are consistent with the approach. For example, looking at timeliness, accuracy, quality, efficiency, or whatever measures the customers say they are interested in. While these factors may not relate directly, they should be directionally correct and consistent with the business mission.

Expense reductions can be a useful measure for calculating rewards, if saving a dollar doesn't mean losing a dollar in profit because of lost revenue. Expense reductions can be viewed favorably by customers (based on their interest in the price of the service) or transparent to the customer. For example, if check processing can be done more efficiently at a cheaper cost, profit may increase and the customer may not be adversely affected.

Where people are involved in activities that may be essential to the long-term viability of the business, the reward should relate to the value of what was accomplished. If a new or enhanced way to profitably meet the customer's needs is found and this new way is to be implemented, we can use the financial dimensions of the return to reward the developers.

Following are some guidelines for putting such a reward system in place.

Define and communicate the bank's commitment to rewarding individuals based on their individual efforts and results. Get as many people as possible into contact jobs and provide them with a customer profitability report to determine how much profit each contact person generates. This can be the basis of the reward system. What precise share everyone gets is less important than the message it sends.

Establish role definitions and personal charters for every bank employee. The roles should relate to the vision, mission, and strategy of the bank and the charters should establish each person's authority and responsibility. The charter should enable everyone to generate profit for the bank.

Develop a plan that outlines each person's activities and results. It should be obvious how these activities will lead to profit, and they should be measurable. The plan may forecast results at a certain level, but the reward system should be open-ended. If the employee exceeds the forecast, the rewards continue.

Analyze the potential range of rewards based on the plan. This gives the employee a sense of what is possible and the bank a sense of the results and expenses. This isn't a promise, but a way to formulate goals in a more concrete fashion.

Determine the level of support, assistance, and training that everyone will need. The plan drives the support, not vice versa. We want to make this as specific as possible so that the support will be available when needed. If there are to be bankwide sales promotion campaigns, the supervisors and the contact staff need to know that because they will make it happen or not happen.

Change the plan as necessary. If external forces such as competition, rates, and new products change the assumptions that went into the plan, change the plan to address these opportunities or conditions. We are looking for profit—not excuses.

Determine the rewards, where possible, on results that are both objectively measurable and controllable by the person to be rewarded. This should be relatively easy for the contact staff, and the same philosophy should apply to other staff. If appropriate rewards cannot be devised, perhaps the goal or plan is not profit- or need-oriented and should be reexamined.

Offer a menu of rewards. As bank customers have different needs, so do bank people. Our reward system must take into consideration what the bank person considers a reward. Some form of monetary compensation should be a choice on the menu. One long-time sales star received relatively good salary increases, won valuable prizes, received publicity and public accolades, but never got the reward that would have meant the most—a promotion and new title.

After outlining the plan to put such a reward system in place, the next step is to think about the range of possible rewards.

The most basic reward or incentive is creating an environment where people enjoy coming to work. It may be some form of human electricity that a culture and people generate. It can be a function of the personal energy of the leaders, a supportive social environment, and the ability to have fun. Whatever it is, we can feel it in a well-managed branch, and so can the customer. Other incentives include:

*Feedback on the job. The One Minute Manager* does a good job of describing how this can be done in an effective, supportive fashion. It is a feeling for people and aiding in their development and growth. The effective manager knows how to do this well. The answer is not withholding feedback that people can use to grow.

*Career employees.* Career employees are usually the heart of a service business; we need to provide continuing incentives that are consistent with profitably satisfying customer needs. The best teller in one branch was a 20-year part-timer. The customers knew she was the best, and so did the branch manager. The problem was that this teller had not received a raise in several years. She was at the maximum and had been told that she would get an increase only if she became a full-time teller. The person didn't want to do this and it was harder to find good part-time staff than full-time staff. This was finally addressed when the notion of a career teller was reintroduced into the bank.

*Career paths.* Years ago most banks had formal career paths and some still do. When someone starts a career in the bank, one of the clear incentives can be a well established career path. This involves more than a time phased system of moving people. It involves enhancing their skills, perhaps by education and training.

But it should be based on their ability, interests, and the bank's needs. Growing people (staff and customers) is usually the most effective way to grow the business.

*Asking for and reacting to staff input.* The staff probably has many good ideas for improving the business but employees have to know management is serious about their contributions.

Rewards can take many forms and as each supervisor works with his or her employees, he or she should find out what would please them. They probably encompass some of the things that we have already mentioned. They also may be a new job for a job well done or they may be interested in helping to develop other people—the stars usually like to do this. By finding out what would please the employees, you will go a long way towards pleasing the customers.

The greatest reward is doing a good job. We have only to ask the stars. The real stars can set the standards for a very long time.

It's hard to be a star if there isn't any work to do, even if you try very hard. If we want people to increase their efficiency, we must ensure there is enough work to make that possible. There are several ways to do that . . .

- Get as many people as possible directly tied to the profit they generate. They will tell you when they need help and what type of help would be most profit-effective.

- Capture the transaction history of each customer to plan capacity needs. For each customer we should record what their transaction history was over the last twelve months, number of visits to branch and type of transaction, number and type of ex-branch service used (ATMs, PC, telephone, mail). This gives us a base level of information to start allocating resources to meet the need.

  In planning new sales campaigns, estimate the effect on transactions. This data and the base transaction levels give us some sense of how much increased efficiency is possible.

- Use cross-training of the staff to get maximum flexibility in meeting fluctuating customer or staff needs. Cross-training is a nice team builder, and it minimizes organizational friction.

- Develop contingency or back-up plans that can be activated as needed without incurring a built-in ongoing cost. Retired employees may help here.

Net, improper staffing is in no one's interest. It's certainly not in the long-term interests of the customers for them to deal with an unproductive bank—it may not be around tomorrow to serve them.

Every manager has an opportunity to make employees entrepreneurs, but it requires a commitment to help people be their best. Once you are committed to them, they will unleash the engine that will drive your bank.

# Chapter 28

# TRAINING: ACQUIRING AND PRACTICING THE NEEDED SKILLS

After we have developed a vision for our bank, we want to define what changes we must make to achieve the vision. We can't forget cultural changes: What opinions, attitudes, and beliefs of both the customers and staff must change?

Once we have identified the required changes, we should describe them in behavioral terms. For example, our vision may suggest selling nontraditional banking products. This in turn may suggest additional product knowledge, sales and service skills, and perhaps learning a new support system (if there are new products involved). After listing all the changes the vision suggests, the next step is to identify who must do the changing—e.g., customers, telephone operators, relationship officers, product specialists, systems people, or management.

Depending on the change and the degree of difficulty of the change, we have two options: We can either find new people (customers or staff) who may already exhibit the behavior we are looking for, or we can train the people we have.

There are six major aspects to consider in developing a training program.

*Culture.* The culture in the bank must say training is important. Viewing training as a means of accomplishing the vision

161

is one way to convey that message. Another way of saying something is important is to participate in it. When Bud Gravette was chairman and CEO of the Bowery Savings Bank, he would often sit in training courses and participate in the discussions, sometimes to the discomfort of the instructor.

The third way is to build culture into the training programs. We can do this by making sure that every new person to the bank learns something about its history, mission, and vision. It should be living history, it should be exciting, and it should describe the social fabric of the bank.

Learning about the culture of an institution provides a vital team-building function. Everyone can benefit, customers included, if we can capture the essence of what the bank stands for and believes in. The Washington Mutual Savings Bank did that with a statement of values in its 1987 annual report.

*The bank's plans.*   One way of introducing a training program is to describe why it's important. Often this can best be done by taking the global vision and mission of the bank and relating it to the specific vision and mission of the people to be trained. Sharing relevant plans is a vehicle for doing this. The detail and scope will depend on the audience, but we should discuss the overall plans and specifically the piece they can impact. The staff member or customer now is in a better position to use the training experience back on the job.

*Specific skills.*   What are the specific skills that will help make the behavioral changes required? How do we best communicate them, learn them, and practice them? Training specialists can help here. They helped train customers to use ATMs.

*Process.*   Very often it isn't a single skill that will be critical in effecting a behavioral change; it is the integration of several new skills that will, for example, help a contact person better meet customers' needs. A training program module could integrate various skills or simply outline how to process customer transactions on a new system.

*Monitoring.*    Training is an investment in achieving the vision and should be carefully monitored to see if the desired change has been accomplished. If we don't, we send a message that training is an optional activity this is not critical to the business.

*A lifelong process.*    Training is not a one-time event—it's a lifelong process in a changing world. Tom Watson, Sr., taught us that. In designing a course, we want to build in this capability with take-home material, an 800 "Help Line," recommended reading, or other courses.

Use Guide 36 as a checklist for evaluating your training program.

---

**GUIDE 36**
**Training Program Checklist**

- What staff or customer need is the training designed to meet?
- What is the scope and level of the training required?
- Is there a clear description of the course with, if possible, feedback from participants?
- Has the course been clearly and openly communicated?
- Is feedback requested from the participants?
- Where possible, is the effect of the course on meeting needs measured?

---

# GATHERING AND ACCESSING THE NEEDED INFORMATION

# Chapter 29

# Monitoring the Execution of the Mission

One day someone came into the office of a senior manager with a pile of computer printout so high it started to wobble. It turned out to be a week's worth of reports designed to help senior management manage the bank. As we began to look at the reports, we noted that:

- The reports were so voluminous it was difficult to believe they were used very often.

- There did not appear any way to determine the relative importance of a report except by reading the whole document.

- The headings and format of the reports were often unintelligible.

- Most of the reports concerned expense, accounting, or operations.

This would have been understandable if the industry was regulated, but it wasn't. The reports were of little value in managing a bank in a deregulated environment. They didn't help answer the question "How are we doing in executing our mission?" The game had changed, but not the score keeping. We need certain information to fulfill the bank's mission to profitably satisfy the customers' financial needs. However, we can capture most of the basic information we need on three concise forms.

The first is a customer service monitoring report (see Guide 37). It's on an individual customer basis and it identifies each product the customer owns, a standard or expected service level, and the actual level delivered. The standards represent the customers' standards, not ours. The test here is What do the customers want? and What are they willing to pay for? One branch spent a fair amount of time monitoring teller waiting time, only to learn that customers' real concern was teller competence. To avoid making a similar mistake, we might want to seek the advice of experts in researching and monitoring customer needs, and we will want to gather and verify this information on a regular basis—every six to eighteen months, for instance. In designing the research, we must ensure that the questions are asked in such a manner that customers respond to both what standard they want (e.g., loan approval) and what they are willing to pay for (e.g., 24 hours or normal business hours).

After we have some reliable information about what standards the customer would set, we have to determine what standards we can profitably meet. This may require going back to the customer or building profitable standards in the original research design. What we would like to wind up with is some basic standards that are few in number so that they can be managed and communicated in a reasonable way. Over time we can fine-tune the mix and the standards. The actual measurement system should be both accurate and timely. The report then becomes more actionable and useful.

Once the report has been produced for a while and appears to be useful, accurate, and timely, we can start using it. Both the contact staff and the customers should get the reports in some form. This gives the contact staff essential information on customer needs, and it gives the customers the message that need satisfaction *is* important (not just profit).

The second report we need is a customer profitability report (see Guide 38). How profitable is each customer based on all the products he or she owns and uses with our bank and the expenses we incur in supplying the product offerings? All customers serviced

## GUIDE 37
## Customer Service Monitoring Report

| Customer Name | Product No. 1 | | Product No. 1 | | Product No. 2 etc. |
|---|---|---|---|---|---|
| | Standard No. 1 | Actual | Standard No. 2 | Actual | |

## GUIDE 38
## Customer Profitability Report

| Customer | Total Accounts | Revenue Based on | | Expenses | | Profit |
|---|---|---|---|---|---|---|
| | | Interest | Fees | Fixed | Variable | |

by a contact person can be grouped together. This lets us compare the profitability of our various contact people so that we can make decisions about staffing and compensation.

This report and the customer service monitoring report tell us how we are doing executing the mission. In time, we may wish to integrate these two reports to capture trend information (e.g., results in last three to six reports). But before we do that, let's use the two reports and get feedback on each.

We also need a market share report to track our share of the consumers' financial service business in our market (see Guide 39).

This report will help us assess our share of the profit in a market. The first line tells us how many customers there are in our market, how many are at our bank, and how many are elsewhere. The second line of the table tells us what the total profit generated in the market is, based on all the customers and all the financial service suppliers they use. The report then breaks down the total between the profit we have and the profit that goes elsewhere. The number on the last line tells us how many suppliers the average household uses.

---

**GUIDE 39**
**Market Share Report**

| | Total Customers | At Our Bank | Elsewhere |
|---|---|---|---|
| Number of Accounts Held | | | |
| Profitability | | | |
| Average Number of Suppliers Used per Customer | | NA | NA |

---

If this report is generated every quarter, we will be able to track our performance in relation to the total growth of the marketplace. If our profit has been growing at a rate of 12 percent and the total market at a rate of 6 percent, we have been doing a good job. If our share of our customers' total profitability has been decreasing, we should find out why. We may be going out of business and not knowing it.

How do we get this report? There may be syndicated market research in our marketplace that we can buy or can research and design our own data gathering systems. The latter may require some outside expertise.

Other reports are also important in managing a consumer bank, but the three reports discussed in this chapter help us understand why we are in business in the first place.

# Chapter 30

# PROVIDING
# OPERATIONAL SUPPORT

One bank had installed a series of processing systems over the years, and they all shared two characteristics: They were in and of themselves designed to be efficient from a processing point of view, and they were not related. They really weren't designed with the customer or user in mind, so it took a fair amount of time to master them. It isn't surprising that the contact staff spent more time processing than selling or serving customers. This encouraged the development over time of a very internally focused culture. It wasn't until a new support manager arrived that the systems and the support culture turned around and focused on the customers. She realized that the systems were not designed to profitably serve customer needs, but only to be expense-efficient.

Whatever our strategy, we will need an operational support system to execute it on a day-to-day basis. It may not be one system per se, but it should be seamless in its use. If it is designed with the customer in mind, it probably will pass the test.

Let's identify the key components of the operating support system.

*A menu of what is available on the system.* Something that the first-time user of the system would be comfortable with.

*Customer information.* A file that contains all the information that the bank knows about the customer—e.g., product ownership, usage, transaction patterns.

*Product information.* A catalogue of the products that the bank sells and the competition. It should describe the benefits and features of the products.

*Processing capability.* Once a sale has been made or after sale service required, this component of the system executes the transaction. If we sell a customer a checking account, what has to happen so that the customer can start using the account? This question relates to the processing capability. Systems should be easy to use, fast, efficient, complete, and above all, designed from the customer/customer contact person's point of view, not from an accounting or data processing point of view.

*Sales tracking.* As a sale is completed and the processing capability is used to execute the sale, we want to make sure that the sale is captured and played back in a sales reporting system. Who sold it? Whom was it sold to? What was the opening profitability?

*Administrative support.* We would like to spend the minimum amount of time on chores that do not relate directly to generating revenue, but are essential to running a business—control, audits, tracking expenses, and ordering supplies. To administer these things efficiently, we have to understand what has to be done and why, and then figure out the best way to do it.

*Data services.* If the bank purchases economic data or consumer market research on a regular basis, there should be some means of accessing this data to serve customers and the entire bank. We need an index so we do not buy the data twice or fail to leverage the original purchase.

173

How do we go about building this capability for our bank? The first thing we should do is identify a branch that has a reputation for being well managed, probably because it has a star branch manager. We want to visit that branch and get a feel for how the successful branch really works, and, of course, understand the operating system that is in place. It's probably a mixture of state-of-the-art and green eyeshade. But it works, as efficiently as the branch manager can make it. The star branch manager does not try to grow his business unless he is sure it is working like a Swiss timepiece.

The branch research will help you do two things. One, define the components of an operating system you think you need. Your commitment is going to be important so make sure you know what and why you need it. Two, a sense of the financial dynamics of each piece of the system. This is the data that will drive the decision to make a component of the system state-of-the-art or green eyeshade. By using the well managed branch as a guide, you can start to understand the value of a good operating system, particularly when you contrast the well managed branch with the poorly managed branch.

Three areas of inquiry will be important to understand: How their expense dollars are spent, how much profit is generated by the branch, and the amount of time the entire branch staff spends on non-revenue producing tasks. Understand these issues and you will be able to play devil's advocate. Ask the question, "Why should I invest in a particular operating system?", and then answer your own question.

Once you have the best operating system in place that can be profit justified, let it run for a while, track the results, and then see how it can be improved. At some point we will probably want to secure the advice of an expert in bank support systems.

As systems are upgraded over time, they may become more complex; that's all right as long as they become easier to use. In evaluating an upgrade to an operating system, we should ask the following questions:

- Is it designed with the customer in mind?

- Is it easy to use?

- Does it have the minimum number of interfaces and steps to accomplish a task?

- Does it have a high degree of accuracy in the processing?

- Is it designed to automatically track work in process?

- Is it timely?

If we stay focused on the customer, we will keep the operating systems issue in the right perspective. All banks have support systems. The key is to make them serve the customers in a profit-effective manner.

The danger here is that someone will say we can't afford it, whatever "it" is, and the bank will trundle along with a series of unrelated and patched up systems that require more and more contact person time (and expertise) to interface with and use. This starts turning the contact staff off who may unconsciously start turning the customers off. It's a recipe for going out of business.

# Chapter 31

# Accessing Information About the Customer

A woman walked into a branch one day and slowly made her way to the teller line. With her unkempt clothing, a cigarette dangling from her mouth, and a far-away look, she seemed out of place in the bank. When she got to the teller, she made her withdrawal and was about to leave when she noticed a sign that described a new account the bank was offering. When she asked about it, the teller said, "Oh, there is a three thousand dollar minimum," with a haughty air of dismissal. The customer went back to her office and called her other bank. They explained that new product in detail, and she decided to purchase one from the proceeds of the business she had recently sold.

If the teller had only looked at her balance and not her dress, the first bank would have gotten the new account. A bank typically has more information about a customer than it uses, probably because it is too expensive to play it back to the contact staff.

We can make the most of the information we have by building a customer file that contains the customer's name, address, balances, and products owned. If the task sounds overwhelming, we could try doing it for the 20 percent of the customers that probably account for 80 percent of the branch's profit. If it works well for them, we can expand it. The type of information we might capture is listed in Guide 40.

# GUIDE 40
## Customer Information File

### Customer

- Date of first account
- Preferred forms of address: Mrs., Dr., etc.
- Telephone number(s)
- Mailing address
- Related customers

### Product

- All products owned
- Current usage level
- Transaction history
- Link to other related accounts

### Service

- Date of CD maturity
- Trust deadline
- Possible educational loan

### Profitability

- Revenue generated by product
- Estimated expense by product
- Total profit generated
- Profitability ranking

The first module is about the customer: date of first account with the bank, titles and addresses of all current accounts open at the bank, list of closed accounts such as paid-up loans, preferred form of address (Mrs., Dr., etc.), and telephone number. Lastly, any other useful information, e.g., small business owner, related to the bank's fourth largest account, medical resident, etc. This module should contain any information that will help us to better understand the customer.

The second module contains information about all the products the customer owns and uses. So if we looked up Mrs. Jones, we would see listed together her checking account, savings account, mutual fund, personal loan, safe deposit, tax preparation, and bank card. We could also determine the usage level of these products—balance, credit outstanding, and taxes prepared for the last five years. The same file should contain any other transactional information such as ATM usage, number of checks written, and number of visits to the bank—in short, a complete transaction history. Let's suppose that Mrs. Jones owns her own business and maintains other business accounts with the bank, is a beneficiary of a trust, or is treasurer of a not-for-profit organization. We will want to note all related accounts to understand how we serve our customers in their various roles.

The third module relates to profitability. It would contain information about the total revenue that Mrs. Jones' relationship generated over the last 12 months, the estimated expense to serve her, the profit generated, and a sense of how profitable Mrs. Jones is to the bank. She might, for instance, be in the top 10 percent of our customers by profitability.

The fourth module would contain any other relevant service information—a reminder before Mrs. Jones' CD matures, Keogh/IRA deadline, tax input due, or trust deadline. This module should contain information that will help the contact person anticipate the customer's needs.

The customer information file should be available to all bank people who have a need to know. It can help contact staff meet

178

customers' needs, it can help market researcher understand the customer, it can help the planner relate needs to plans to execution, and it can help managers track/understand the business.

How do we capture this information? Let's ask a few successful salespeople what they know about their customers and how they learned it. They know more about their customers than Guide 39 suggests, and they got most of the information by listening. They recorded the information in their head and on a three-by-five file card.

The first step, then, is to get all the contact staff listening, recording, and using the information they have about the customer. Once we have done that, we can identify what else the bank knows and start playing this information back to the contact staff. When we have all the information filtering back to the contact staff, we can then try to make it easier for the contact staff to use the information either by formatting it in some useful fashion or performing some standard calculations such as individual customer profitability. This will probably require some expert assistance, but if we take it a step at a time we can build a customer information file that is used by the contact staff to profitably satisfy customers' needs.

Some people might say it is too expensive to maintain a customer information file, but can you be in the deregulated financial service business without it?

# Chapter 32

# HELPING THE CUSTOMER DECIDE

Some day, sit down at your desk—the one you would see a customer at—and write down all the products that your bank sells. You can use whatever reference material you have and make whatever telephone calls you wish to complete your list. Keep track of how long this takes. When you are finished, show your list to people in marketing, operations, or auditing and see if they can identify any other products.

The next step is to identify how many key features each account has. How many pieces of information on prices and rules of use would you need to communicate the features of the account to a customer? If this process takes a long time, you have your first piece of valuable information: Product information is not easily accessible. If necessary, estimate the number of features. Don't forget to include all the variations, e.g., various mortgage products.

Now get out the telephone book and list every financial service company you can identify, including banks, insurance companies, brokerage firms, investment advisers, and check cashers. Estimate the number of products and features each one has.

Multiply all the numbers and you will get the approximate number of data elements a customer in your area might have to be familiar with to make informed financial decisions. The number is probably in excess of 10,000. How long did it take you to do this—

several hours or several days? And remember, you were merely counting, not necessarily understanding. This suggests that the typical customer does not thoroughly examine all his or her choices. Well, suppose we could somehow help with this process?

A product information system like the one in Guide 41 provides specific information about the products we sell and those of our competitors. It can enable the contact person to help the customer make an informed product choice.

The first component of the system contains information about all consumer products sold. A description of the product, a list of needs it can meet for the customer, benefits of using the product, the price (interest rate, fees, other charges), terms of sale, product options, and whom to contact for more information.

---

**GUIDE 41**
**Product Information System**

- Consumer Products
  —description
  —rates
  —benefits
  —terms
  —whom to contact for more information

- Other Bank Products
  —same information as above, but condensed
  —leading to right salesperson

- Competitive Information
  —similar to above

- Standard Financial Calculation
  —net present value, amortization, etc.

- Processing Information
  —a road map on how to execute sales or service

---

The second component contains the same type of information for nonconsumer products the bank sells, such as business loans, leasing arrangements, and venture capital. Here the information may be briefer, as long as it is enough to get the customer hooked up to the right person. We need to make sure that we don't lose customers because we are not familiar with all the bank's products.

The third component contains competitive information. It's hard for anyone to help customers meet their financial needs if one does not at least have a general sense of what the customer's options are. The information can be used to convey a sense of professionalism to the customer. It also can crystallize what differences in rate mean. For example, a 1/4% on a CD for the amount of money the customer might deposit could equate to $4 per month; this may be less than the customer thought it was and puts the decision in different perspective. A comparison of similar products in the marketplace may result in a feature that is very important to the customer that only your bank has. This competitive information should be similar to the information described above and structured in a way that facilitates comparison and pop differences.

The fourth component is standard financial calculations. The system should have the ability to calculate the four-dollar difference mentioned above as well as the size of monthly payments for an auto loan. If a calculation could be used frequently to help customers, it probably should be included here.

The fifth component is a processing road map: Once you have made the sale, what do you do? What forms have to be filled out? What other documents are required? Where do they go? How can you follow up on the processing or ask questions?

The whole idea of the product information system is to make it as easy as possible for the contact person to profitably satisfy the customer needs. This and the potential volume of data make it essential to secure professional assistance in structuring the data. The contact person should be able to zero in on the information he or she wants and then pick the level of detail desired or identify a follow-up contact or referral person.

How do we start to manage this process? After all, the bank does have information available.

First, we talk to a cross-section of our contact staff and find out how they are currently handling this problem. We should emerge with a sense of possible ways to improve the process and the value of doing so. Specifically, we would like to identify the most likely products to work on first, based on frequency of sale or the profitability of the product versus the opportunity to improve profit by increasing access to product information. In the process of doing this, we may discover some informal systems the contact staff uses. Let's take three or four of the most likely opportunities and see what we can do with them. We can, with the contact staff's help, structure the information in a usable format and then ask them to start using it, noting what customers or prospective customers they use it for and any hints to improve it. We will want to use the information that we have put together for awhile not only to get feedback, but to identify how we can best keep the information updated and how needed it really is.

If we can identify a means of increasing profitability for three or four products, we can expand our base and seek out ways to gather and disseminate the data more easily. We are not looking for the most sophisticated system, only the one that helps us profitably satisfy our customers' needs.

Banks invest in products to satisfy customers' needs; we want to make sure that all relevant information about the products is available at point of contact to make that investment pay off. The myriad of facts and figures concerning a consumer bank's products, as well as its competitors, requires a simple system to access this information. This will permit us to leverage our investment in the products we develop.

# CULTURE
# CAN KILL

# Chapter 33

# DIAGNOSING YOUR CULTURE

Culture is not something that grows overnight. Understanding how it developed in consumer banking may help us better understand and manage it. Let's see if we can identify some of the cultural threads in the consumer banking business.

The long years of regulation had many effects; one was the reactive nature of the position banks were in. In a sense they reacted both to regulation and to the customer. If you are in this mode long enough, it becomes very difficult to do anything else. So things like customer focus, innovation, aggressively asking a customer for his business, although in theory simple enough to do, are against the cultural grain.

Over the past twenty years or so, many commercial bank branches were reorganized and had a lot of things taken away from them, from customers to operations to a clear branch role. This created a defensive attitude on the part of the branches and a second class connotation towards working in the branches. This one fact is probably the key to understanding why the culture is so hard to change.

For many years there was a strong hierarchical organization in the branches; this helped to create a strong class/clan system. Many different groups were spawned, but the common element was lack of true teamwork; groups like the tellers versus the platform staff, officers versus nonofficers, vice presidents versus other officers,

187

operation versus the branches. To expect the culture to change just because the industry was deregulated ignores the strength of the culture.

Stories that would seem absurd in one culture become perfectly reasonable in another. Let's take the case of a branch that had just been renovated; the staff noticed a strange, persistent smell now present, similar to that in a dry cleaning store. Repeated calls to the general services organization produced no action, and the branch felt that no one cared. Finally a customer complained to the president of the bank, and that achieved some action. The smell was caused by a problem in the air-conditioning system.

The culture in this case did not support its business and did not encourage the various units of the bank to support one another on a basic, common need—health and safety.

When is culture a problem? When it is not in sync with the business or, worse, when it doesn't support basic needs of all people. When these things happen it's usually obvious, but can we somehow identify the danger signs of culture and do something about them in advance of a problem? Guide 42 is a checklist for you to use in diagnosing your culture.

Any signs of cultural danger may be subject to different interpretations, but if most of the signs show red, we may have a cultural problem. How can we create a culture that is in sync with the business, the times, and the environment?

- Relate the effects of culture on profit in managing the bank

- Training

- Restructuring the business

- Infusion of new people

- Encourage interaction with select people outside the bank

- Keep asking, "What would the customer say?"

## GUIDE 42
### Diagnosing Your Culture

1. *Inner focus of staff.* Carlzon talked about the introverted staff. The focus could be a process, but in the worst case the staff tends to focus on itself, as if to say, "If only the customer would go away." Customers can sense this, and so can good managers.

2. *Process is paramount.* Process is very important, but it exists to meet a customer need. So if the focus and measurement system are on process, the bank is making a statement about what is *not* being focused on—the customer.

3. *Class/clan system.* This problem is usually observable when one bank employee interacts with another or doesn't interact with another. It may appear to be lack of caring, "bureaucracy," or poor teamwork. Also, the respect or indifference they show one another may be a clue.

4. *Customers are not looked to for input.* This can be discerned both as an attitude and as a failure to communicate. Does management make decisions on which a prudent person would want direct customer input, or does management simply not ask the customer?

5. *Resistance to change.* Listening to how people react to suggestions can be helpful here. When a course of action is obvious but still is not taken, the culture might be saying, "That's not the way we do things." Resistance to change is often a predisposition that becomes obvious over time.

6. *Ingrown staff.* This symptom will be fairly obvious by the similarity of the staff's background and views. In an industry that is experiencing great change, a mix of people usually works best.

7. *Failure is not used as a learning experience.* There is only one redeeming feature to failure, and that is that it presents an opportunity to learn something

that may prevent another failure. If this opportunity is missed—if someone is singled out for unusual punishment, or the failure is covered up—it may signal a cultural problem.

8. *A tendency towards pessimism.* If the organization expects the worst to happen, it usually does and no one is surprised. This can be obvious in the most trivial conversations. Customers can usually feel it, too.

9. *Low risk tolerance.* The test here may be as simple as analyzing what happened to the last person who failed. If there isn't one in a rapidly changing environment, it may be because no one is even trying to react to the changes. If there is one, and the last person is in corporate Siberia, the message is that taking risks does not pay.

10. *Lack of fun.* If the atmosphere in the bank is generally somber, this may be a clue that fun isn't allowed. Very few organizations can operate at the limits of their potential without a sense of fun and excitement.

But there must be a critical mass of these types of things if new initiatives are to have a permanent effect on culture. Otherwise the voice crying in the wilderness will soon be silenced. Culture can be changed, but it's hard work and it takes a long time. The danger with culture is that it can kill ideas, kill people, and slowly kill an organization.

# Chapter 34

# Developing a
# Sales Culture

John Smith managed most of the branches for the bank. He was a practitioner of the Peters and Waterman notion of managing by walking around. One day, John was visiting a branch that he kept a concerned eye on. He slowly passed the tellers and then approached the platform area. He walked by two empty desks and stood directly in front of the third desk. The person at that desk didn't look up until John put his hand on the desk. The platform officer finally looked up and said, "Oh, Mr. Smith, I thought you were a customer!"

The first thing that we have to do to increase sales is not to send someone to a sales training course, but to ask ourselves if a sales culture exists in our bank. If it does, we will feel it and observe it. It will permeate the organization. If we do not pick up these signals, there probably isn't strong emphasis on sales in the culture. But there are some specific questions we can ask:

What do most of the people in the bank seem to focus on? If it's process, clubs, or reorganizations, this may be the first sign that customers aren't important.

What is the perception of how to succeed in the bank? This subject is usually uppermost in the mind of new persons to an organization, so observing them may help. If a significant part of the answer to this question does not relate to profit or sales, this may be the second sign.

Where in the bank are the rewards greatest? Where do the "savvy" people gravitate to? If the answer is not in large measure to customer contact areas, you should at least understand why. It may be that sales are not presumed to be important.

What are the rewards for? If rewards seem to be frequently associated with control activities or fixing problems, what rewards are left for profit?

Do priorities often get changed? If there seems to be a new priority every quarter, that may be a sign that confusion or lack of commitment is driving the culture, not sales or anything else. Sales requires a long-term commitment as we will see, so turning it on and off will not work.

Who gets promoted? By looking at the background and track record, it may be possible to discern a pattern here. It may be the old boy network, a functional specialty (operations?), internal promotions, or external hires. Whatever it is, it's probably a clue.

If the answers to the above questions don't include sales, there is a problem. The first thing to do is probably to start focusing your colleagues on the customer. Personal example is a good start. After the spotlight has been turned on the customers, it is time to send three simple messages·

- Customers are valued.

- The bank wants more of their customers' business.

- We would like our customers to think of us as their bank.

When these become the shared values of the organization, we have met the preconditions for a sales culture. Unless they exist, money spent on sales will be money poorly invested.

How do we build a sales culture? There are a number of specific things we can do, including:

*Sales Goals.* There should be specific sales goals for each person involved in selling. They should be realistic and reflective of the opportunity the bank has to make money.

*Training.* Sales training should be a long-term commitment. For most people, sales skills can always be improved and as there are new products developed and new support systems, training becomes a vehicle to grow and achieve a vision.

*Sales Support.* It's essential that all the tools to support a sale are in place, including applications, brochures, and disclosures. This also includes customer information and product information.

*Sales Execution.* Once a sale has been made, can it be efficiently executed? I remember one product where new accounts never seemed to wind up on the computer. It turned out to be an editing problem. The point is, don't turn off the sales people by making it difficult for them to execute a sale.

*Sales Tracking.* Sales should be effortlessly and accurately tracked. If a system can handle accounting, it should be able to handle sales tracking. The tracking has to be at the customer and salesperson level. Also, the feedback should be ASAP to be most useful.

*Sales Incentives.* They are essential to sending the message that we are serious about our mission of profitably serving customers' needs. It is important that the rewards relate to profitability and need satisfaction.

*Sales Coaching.* There are sales stars in any organization, and usually they are very pleased to share their experiences and ideas. We want to leverage this resource so the entire sales staff can benefit. It may be sales meetings, role playing, or team selling. If we have the prerequisites in place and support them with specifics, we have the start of a sales culture. With some cheerleading from senior management, we may have something that we can grow. But anything that grows needs constant attention.

There are several signs we can look for to determine if our sales culture is growing. First, salespeople put themselves in their customers' shoes and in doing this they sell need-satisfying solutions. Not what the bank is pushing, but what the customer needs. Second, sales stars never sell anything they are not sure works. They understand how it works and what the potential problems are, so they are in a position to help the customer. Third, the experienced sales person never over-promises. If anything, there is a tendency to under-promise and over-deliver to build a long-term relationship with a customer. Selling isn't doing any one thing well, it's making sure that all the interrelated components to selling are in place and working together. But you start by building a sales culture.

# Chapter 35

# CUSTOMER COMMUNICATIONS

A very profitable customer was talking to the branch manager. She was asking him to "explain" what the letter she was holding should mean to her. The letter was really quite clear. It said that there would be some reductions in service.

"Does that mean I can't continue to conduct my banking over the telephone?" said the customer.

"Oh no, this letter doesn't apply to you. You can continue to bank as you always have."

"But why did you send the letter to me?" she said.

The letter was sent because the bank did not differentiate among customers when it communicated with them. The customer knew that was the reason because she had raised the issue before. On one occasion a senior executive told her that they had too many customers to know each one of them.

This is unfortunate for at least two reasons. One, there is a wide spread in household profitability among customers. The high profit customer in one survey was *thirteen* times as profitable as the marginal customer (see Guide 9). Second, most customers have some additional profit to bring to a bank; the last thing we want to do is discourage them from doing so by sending them the message we don't care enough about you as a customer to send you the right message.

Communications is like any other investment we make in a customer. The prudent investor is not expense-driven but recognizes an opportunity and invests accordingly.

In order to tailor our communication we need information about the customer and a customer communications system that is responsive to the contact staff. The former helps us identify the profitability of the customer and any other useful information. (e.g., Is it Ms. Jones, Dr. Jones, or Mrs. Jones?) The latter helps the contact staff to tailor the communication to the customer.

Generally speaking, we will want the person in the bank who is the customer's primary contact to be the one who communicates with the customer. They should know the customers best and know what the bank can profitably do for them. But the primary customer contact person needs additional management support.

First, a clear statement that the goal of a customer communication is to help the customers better meet their needs and generate profitability for the bank, in contrast to, for example, what the bank wants to say.

Second, training in good communications—verbal, nonverbal (body language, for example), in writing. Communicating should be done with care, and it requires training and practice.

Third, support. This might be a telephone, a word processor, or something else the contact person can control. It might be guidelines on when and how to communicate, a set of basic letters that the customer contact person can modify as needed, or a hotline to get help in writing a letter.

Fourth, a tracking system that helps the contact person follow up and initiate communications on a timely basis. Every letter to the customer should build on what we know about the customer.

If we have the customer information available and the ability for each contact staff member to communicate directly with customers, we should provide some guidelines on how to communicate.

*Whom are we trying to communicate with?* If it's only safe-deposit customers, then that narrows the field. If it's all customers, to announce a promotion, that's another story. Or it may be one customer to send a thank-you letter to. The star salesperson always sends thank-you letters. It's an opportunity to maintain contact.

*Do we know how best to communicate with that customer?* One sales star made it a practice to send a letter to her customers that said, "I have something that may interest you. Please call when you have a chance." ATM users might not even realize that they have a contact person.

*Why are we communicating?*    Is it a legal requirement or news of a new product or information about the bank? The reason drives not only the content, but also the style. If we know something about the customer's product ownership, usage, or transaction pattern, we may be able to make the relevance to the particular customer more apparent.

*What do we want to say?*    If it's a fairly complex message, we want to make sure it's said in as clear a fashion as possible. Perhaps we are trying to say too much. Whatever it is, we should be able to headline it in our mind and use that as the focus of our thoughts.

*Is there something we want the customer to do?*    If the answer is yes, what is it? Let's make it clear what the customer should do and how to do it. If it's communicating a new telephone number, perhaps the inclusion of a business or wallet card would help. If it requires another type of action, perhaps a reply card or an application is needed. In this case let's make it as easy as possible by filling in all relevant information we know. Perhaps a telephone call will suffice.

*Are there any legal implications?*    Much of what we write has legal implications, so we want to have legal counsel review it. But we don't want lawyers to write it unless it is absolutely necessary.

*Is there a time limit for the person to reply?*    If so, let's make it clear. We are not trying to lay mine fields for our customers or ourselves.

*Have we used whatever resources are appropriate to help us communicate?*    For the customers we see or talk to on a regular basis, a note on our calendar or follow-up list may suffice. If it's a thank-you, a short, personal note may be all we need to think about. A direct marketing program, on the other hand, may involve multiple communications with various pieces of supporting material. The sign-up rate becomes a critical variable. In this case it might be wise to invest in expert help. If someone has a good track record in this area, we should at least talk to that person.

*Have we tested the communication?* What we communicate and what people perceive are two different things. So while the effectiveness of our communication may be measured by our success rate or profit, we want to ensure that the reader or listener understands what we communicated. If the communication is in person, we may get some clues that we can react to or we may be able to ask questions or say it another way. With written communications we usually have one change, so if it's important, we should pretest our written communications by asking a select group of customers questions about the communication to see if the message was received and how we can improve it.

A bank was preparing a letter that described a new service; when it pretested the letter, it found that there were two or three paragraphs that the readers ignored. It wasn't that they didn't understand them, but merely that the information was not useful. The bank felt that eliminating those paragraphs increased the response rate.

Communication may not be a science, but it is not a process either; it is a major vehicle for changing behavior. The manner in which we communicate reflects our culture. Make it customer focused!

# Chapter 36

# MATCHING THE WORDS AND THE ACTION

A bank introduced a new product and spent a lot of money putting together an elaborate marketing program. To judge by the creative aspects of the communications program, it should have been a success. The customer had a need and the communication material explained it clearly and effectively to the customer. The contact staff were introduced to the new product, but there wasn't any efficient way to execute the sale; the contact staff didn't have applications, and the processing system wasn't very effective. The problems were addressed as they were discovered during the roll out, but not without a cost in poor morale and lost sales. This happened with other new products and the result was an undermining of the commitment. It took a new management team to get the consistency between words and action sorted out.

The solution was fairly simple. It required:

- A clear understanding—before the introduction of new products—of what was required and how long it would take to achieve a favorable result.

- A detailed plan of how to successfully introduce the product with milestones that were carefully and regularly monitored by everyone, including senior management.

- A contingency plan that anticipated some of the problems.

- A system to gather crucial feedback quickly and fix the problems.

- A review, once a steady state was achieved, to discuss and document lessons learned for other roll outs.

Let's step back for a minute and think about why inconsistencies develop in an organization. It's not by design, for few people are anarchists at heart.

Often the problem is not perceived; management has taken a series of actions, perhaps over time and seemingly unrelated, that when taken together spell inconsistency. Viewing banking as a system—Principle 1—can help here.

Inconsistencies may be the result of changing priorities. We all change focus on occasion, but sometimes we don't allow enough time and communications effort to bridge the gap. The Titanic principle helps here: The larger the vessel or the larger the enterprise, the more time it takes to change course.

Sadly, inconsistencies may also be a result of lack of commitment on the part of the bank or its senior management. This problem can be solved only by commitment, and that requires:

- A clearly communicated vision, mission, and charter for each employee.

- The presence of the basic tools of the consumer banking business—at least an operating support system. Information about the customer, product information, and basic branch resources.

- The presence of a strategy and a detailed execution plan. The plan should be a living document that changes as more information feedback becomes available. Planning in part is a learning experience.

- Visible management. Management can show support in a substantive fashion as decisions are made and resources are allocated, but management also should walk around and talk to the staff and customers.

How can we tell if consistency is a problem? There are countless signs, but some of the more common are:

- Sales are important but there is no real training, support, or reward system.

- Cross-selling is important but it's not measured either by customer or seller.

- Credit is an important product, but it's hard to process loans even with full collateral.

- Service is important, but the customer contact staff are managed as if they were an expense.

- Service is important, but the business is driven by process.

- Relationship marketing is important, but customer information isn't available.

- There is a profit focus, but individual customer profitability does not exist.

- Service is important, but it's not measured.

If you observe these signs, the best approach is to surface them in a nonconfrontational manner. This can be done by describing the elements of an issue that are not in sync. "I don't understand . . ." Some of the other approaches mentioned in this chapter may be of help. Tracking the action or idea in question back to the mission may help. Inconsistency is a problem that must be fixed because it creates a noise level in communication with staff and customer, can undermine sales and morale, and may render an investment worthless.

# Chapter 37

# SETTING THE STANDARDS

The main railroad station in one city was an old building constructed in an elegant cathedral style. Due to declining traffic, the station had fallen into disrepair over the years. The only people in the station now were the ones who had to be there. The visitors admiring its classic beauty had stopped coming—except for one person: the president of the local bank.

The president was born in a day when it was not unusual for a young boy to want to be a railroader, and he did. Almost every day at lunchtime he would walk through the terminal and say hello to the janitor, who had been there longer than the bank president had been with the bank. One day the president remarked how clean the terminal was despite the general neglect in other areas. He knew it was due to the efforts of the janitor; no one else cared. The janitor said there were problems getting supplies but he knew how to make do. He then said something the bank president never forgot. He said, "I keep the terminal clean because that's the way it should be." It was a question of a personal standard.

As the president walked back to the bank that day he wondered what would happen if everyone in the bank felt as the janitor did. Every person who comes into contact directly or indirectly with a customer in the bank has the ability to set his or her own standards and meet them. How can we foster this attitude in our bank?

- We can select people who want to be in the service business.

- We can support them with the bank's basic systems and culture. The systems can provide the tools, and a culture that focuses on the customers can cultivate the right mind-set in the staff.

- We can make sure that the service stars receive the praise they deserve and that their accomplishments are communicated to staff, customers, and the general public—orchestrated adulation.

- We can offer one service award each quarter; with the award might go a check, but the focus is on the award.

- Witnessing . . . Instead of the manager being the only one to talk about the importance of setting and maintaining the standards to the bottom line, get the contact people to talk about their experience where good service brought them new business.

- We can involve the contact staff in setting the standards. They are the most knowledgeable about what customers expect and what the bank can profitably do. We also want their commitment in meeting the standards. Standards that are never met, like races that are never won, do not reinforce a winning culture.

- We can put some fun into the work we do. People will normally be more efficient and productive if they enjoy what they do. This is particularly true in the service business, where feelings and attitudes are visible to the customers.

# Chapter 38

# Providing
# Cultural Support

One branch never seemed to have problems with tellers. The turnover was lower than at other branches, and the positive feedback from customers was far above average. Losses, overtime, and salary and benefit expenses were lower than one might expect. It was well known that the branch manager was a star, but what magic she used with the tellers was a mystery. The secret was the great care she took in individually managing each teller. It started with screening her tellers and conducting a thorough initial interview where she took great care to explain what the branch was about, how it differed from other branches, and what its culture was like. The person being interviewed also spoke with several other people in the branch. The normal teller training program was augmented by more information about the bank and the branches, its plans, and how the teller would fit in. In time, the teller was cross-trained in other jobs in the branch.

But what really made the difference was that the manager found out what would please the teller and, within her power, worked with the teller to achieve those goals. They varied, but often it was education or a career path. The manager worked within the bank guidelines to help the person plan an educational development program. When the teller was ready for the next career step, the manager was again there to help. Sometimes the issue was flexible hours. Again, within the needs of the business, this was accommodated because all the tellers were trained to work as a team.

Where possible, any rewards that the branch manager received were shared with the branch. Occasionally the manager would run a sales contest with prizes such as a day off or hold a turkey raffle at the holiday season. In-bank training programs were also used to reward the tellers by allowing them to acquire new developmental skills.

The manager had a philosophy about her team, and part of it was taking care of them. She recognized the golden opportunity that most people missed—the opportunity to manage people in a way that encouraged them to do their best. She had, in fact, developed her own personnel support system, and it worked very well. How can we develop one for the bank? Probably you have a start with your employee benefits program, but let's identify the other major components of a support system.

*Financial partner.*   The bank can be a financial partner with the staff member by providing life insurance, medical insurance, disability insurance, subsidized meals, education, and day care. It might be most equitable to offer each staff member a menu of benefits to choose from.

*Career counseling and training.*   These are two specific areas in which the bank can help staff members realize their goals and build a more profit-effective bank. A program for tellers that has a specific career path and a commitment to their education is an example of such a program.

*Information.*   Health related information, tax information, information on governmental assistance programs, cultural events, and job postings can be made available to all staff members.

*Grants to community organizations.*   Banks can also provide support to community organizations that may in turn benefit bank employees. These include libraries, health care facilities, and counseling programs. Banks can encourage the staff to do the same with a matching grant program.

*Networking assistance.* An employee who is dealing with a problem such as a sick parent may need someone to talk to or put them in touch with resources. The bank can help by maintaining a list of network associations.

*Feedback and coaching.* The staff and the bank can both benefit by situation-specific feedback and coaching. When someone does a good job or there is a way to do the job better, feedback or coaching concurrent with the situation is most effective.

There are other components of a personnel support system that can be custom tailored for your bank. You can get some insights and ideas by talking to benefit suppliers and the customers—in this case, the bank employees. Well-designed research, to identify a range of support items with some sense of their relative importance, is vital in designing an effective support system. You are trying to satisfy employees' needs, not what you think their needs are, and you want to do it in a way that allows the employees to choose what's best for them.

After you have designed your own system, you can use Guide 43 as a checklist. As the checklist suggests, you need the commitment of your managers to make this work. That's why the branch manager in our story was so effective.

The danger here is that the personnel support system will be regarded as a low priority, implying that people don't count. The service business depends upon people, and everyone who owns a service business knows that.

> Treat the staff well,
> They will treat the customer well,
> And the customer will treat you well.

---

### GUIDE 43
### Personnel Support System Checklist

- Do the employees know what the personnel support system is and what it contains?

- Where possible, do the employees have a choice of support system services?

- Does the bank utilize its philanthropic resources where possible to focus on the customers and staff?

- Does each manager have a development plan for each person?

- Does each manager's charter contain a development responsibility and authority?

- Is each manager personally and emotionally committed to the people that he or she works with?

- Is employee feedback a regular and utilized component of the support system?

---

# EPILOGUE

There is a theme to managing a consumer bank and it can be summed up in two words: profit and needs. Consumers are looking for a way to meet their financial needs. From their point of view, it is the relationship between what they pay for the products and services and what return they receive on that investment. For transactional products like a checking account it may simply be the least expensive cost coupled with efficiency, accuracy and timeliness. For investment products it may be return coupled with advice that will meet their other needs like risk and access to their funds. Depending on the need, consumers' perceptions will vary; hence what constitutes good service will vary.

Banks may have a simpler definition of profitability. It may be making a profit on their investments in meeting consumers' needs. The test is a fairly straightforward one in concept but in practice can best be accomplished by applying this test of profitability to each customer individually rather than as a group. A bank may incur less expense to profitably satisfy the needs of the low profit group of consumers than it would to satisfy the high profit consumers. Managing expenses—as important as that is—is not the name of the game. It's managing profit.

Customers have needs, and while all customers share some common needs, some customers have a broader array of needs. But whatever they are, the win for the supplier is to determine how to satisfy those needs in a profit-effective manner that the consumer will pay for. This is in part a function of understanding the customers and their needs and in part creatively satisfying those needs and convincing the consumer that it passes the test for them. ATMs are a good example of this marriage because they represented an innovation that was potentially good for both parties in a changing environment. That kind of innovation must continue if banks are to survive and prosper.

This book has identified seven essential principles for successfully managing a consumer bank and specific guides for doing this. The fly in the ointment is resistance to change on the part of both consumers and banks. Potential dangers have been identified in the various chapters with specific thoughts on how to overcome them. The biggest danger is in the culture of the banks. Consumers have financial needs that won't go away. If banks were organizations of entrepreneurs, they would find a way to profitably serve their customers on a continuing basis; otherwise as individual entrepreneurs they would be out of business. Organizations of employees, on the other hand, often have other issues to address, such as keeping a job. These issues may not be consonant with meeting customers' needs. Management's challenge, then, is to direct the resources of the firm so that both the customers' and the employees' needs are met in a way that produces a viable business over time. Management can do this by supplying a clear mission statement for the business—i.e., profitably satisfying customers' needs —and then building an organization and a culture that support it. Feedback from the customers and monitoring individual customer profitability become essential.

The recipe is simple, but unless you are already there, it becomes a matter of managing change. A culture that recognizes and encourages change is an essential first step in managing change. An acceptance of prudent risk taking is another. The need to change does not presuppose what and how to change. This is where leadership and risk taking come in. Much has been written about leadership, the need for vision, effective communications, commitment building, emotional energy, personal example, and support of others. But there is another quality—trust. Unless

210

the followers believe the leader will be there to support them on the journey, they naturally will act to protect themselves, and this may not be consistent with achieving the vision.

One man ran his own bank successfully for many years. It was in every sense in a class by itself, and when he retired his successor asked him what his secret was. He thought a moment and replied that he focused on the customers and supported the people who generated the revenue. He said that what differentiated him from his peers was one word . . . focus. Everyone talked about the customers and some even talked about supporting the revenue producers, but he really did it.

# BIBLIOGRAPHY

Albrecht, Karl and Zemke, Ron. *Service America.* Dow Jones-Irwin, 1985.

Barnard, Chester I. *The Functions of the Executive.* Harvard University Press, 1938.

Bennis, Warren and Nanus, Burt. *Leaders: The Strategy for Taking Charge.* Harper & Row, 1985.

Carlzon, Jan. *Moments of Truth.* Ballinger, 1987.

Crosby, Philip B. *Quality Is Free.* McGraw-Hill, 1979.

Dale, Ernest. *Readings in Management.* McGraw-Hill, 1965.

Hopkins, Tom. *How to Master the Art of Selling.* Warner, 1982.

Johnson, Spencer and Blanchard, Kenneth. *The One Minute Manager.* Morrow, 1984.

Katz, Daniel and Kahn, Robert L. *The Social Psychology of Organizations.* Wiley, 1966.

Lovelock, Christopher F. *Managing Service Marketing.* Prentice-Hall, 1988.

Maslow, A. H. *Motivation and Personality.* Harper & Row, 1954.

McGregor, Douglas. *The Human Side of Enterprise.* McGraw-Hill, 1960.

Norman, Richard. *Service Management.* Wiley, 1984.

Peters, Thomas J. and Waterman, Jr., Robert H. *In Search of Excellence.* Warner, 1984.

Townsend, Robert. *Further Up The Organization.* Knopf, 1984.

# INDEX